Alcohol and Entertainment Licensing: A Practical Guide

Second Edition

ERRATUM:

LATE NIGHT LEVY AND EARLY MORNING
RESTRICTION ORDERS

The Late Night Levy (Expenses, Eexmptions and
Reductions) Regulations 2012 and The Licensing Act
2003 (Early Morning Retriction Orders) Regulations
2012 have confirmed the provisional proposals as
outlined on pages 110 to 116.

The Early Morning Restriction Order Regulations make
it clear that people have 42 days to make
representations on a proposed order; the hearing must
commence no later than 30 working days after the end
of the 42 day period; the authority can adjourn a
hearing to consider representations made by a party or
if it is in the public interest to do so; any decision must
be made within 10 working days after the end of the
hearing. No later than 7 days after making the decision
to make an EMRO the authority must send a copy of
the decision to all licence holders affected, publish the
EMRO on its website and advertise the order in the
affected area.

Alcohol and Entertainment Licensing: A Practical Guide

Second Edition
David A Chambers and Roger Butterfield

SWEET & MAXWELL

 **THOMSON REUTERS**

First Edition   2006   by David A Chambers and Roger Butterfield (published by Shaw & Sons)

Second Edition   2012   by David A Chambers and Roger Butterfield

Published in 2012 by Sweet & Maxwell, 100 Avenue Road, London, NW3 3PF part of Thomson Reuters (Professional) UK Limited (Registered in England & Wales, Company No 1679046.
Registered Office and address for service: Aldgate House, 33 Aldgate High Street, London, EC3N 1DL)

Sweet & Maxwell ® is a registered trademark of Thomson Reuters (Professional) UK Limited.

For further information on our products and services, visit *www.sweetandmaxwell.co.uk*

Typeset by Letterpart Ltd, Reigate, Surrey

Printed and bound in Great Britain by CPI Group (UK) Ltd, Croydon, CR0 4YY

No natural forests were destroyed to make this product; only farmed timber was used and re-planted.

A CIP catalogue record of this book is available for the British Library.

ISBN: 978-0-414-04488-3

Preface

The Licensing Act 2003 has only been in force since 2005 but respective Governments have amended the legislation is various ways. The introduction of summary reviews, the addition of the licensing authority as a Responsible Authority, the removal of the "vicinity test", licensing authorities no longer needing to be satisfied it is "necessary" to take action but decide it is "appropriate" to do so. The Police Reform and Social Responsibility Act 2011 also introduced Early Morning Restriction Orders and the Late Night Levy. This edition deals with all these changes and sets out the procedures for introducing EMROs and the Late Night Levy.

As well as legislative changes there have been a number of High Court decisions considering issues such as adjournments, appeals, costs. All the relevant cases are considered in the book.

The Licensing Act 2003–An Overview

Introduction

In the licensing world all was chaos, confusion and great darkness. A voice spoke into the darkness saying, "Take heart, things could be worse but take courage for I have come to your aid". So the great god DCMS[1] laboured mightily and brought forth the Licensing Act 2003 and lo, things were indeed much, much worse.

This is probably unfair, as there is no doubt that the licensing regime that the Act replaced was a total mess. It was riddled with anomalies and there were some 40 different licences or permissions to sell alcohol or provide entertainment. The system was long overdue for reform.

However, even before the Act became law it was described as a minefield. Since the first edition of this book was published there have been several significant amendments and it likely there will be more to come. There have also been a number of High Court decisions on the legislation. This book aims to guide the practitioner safely through this ever changing minefield in the simplest way possible.

This book does not seek to be a weighty legal tome but a straightforward and practical guide to the legislation.

---

[1]   Department for Culture, Media and Sport.

Definitions

Throughout this book:

- "the Act" refers to the Licensing Act 2003;
- "section" (s.) refers to a section of the Licensing Act 2003;
- "Regulations" refer to Regulations made under the Licensing Act 2003; and
- "statutory guidance" refers to guidance issued by the Secretary of State.
- "2011 Act" refers to the Police Reform and Social Responsibility Act 2011
- "2012 Act" refers to the Live Music Act 2012.

Aims of the legislation

The stated aim of the Act was to modernise and integrate the various licensing systems in England and Wales and to replace them with a simpler, transparent and accountable system. The goal was to help to build a fair and prosperous society that properly balances the rights of people and their communities. Finally, it aspired to ensure integration with other government initiatives, in order to:

(i)   reduce crime and disorder;
(ii) encourage tourism;
(iii) reduce alcohol misuse;
(iv) encourage the self-sufficiency of local communities; and
(v)   reduce the burden of unnecessary regulation on business.

Whether these aims were achieved is another matter. Certainly, the new licensing regime is an integrated one; whether it has proved to be simpler is doubtful, particularly when it is considered that the Act is so large and has been amended several times. It has 9 Parts, 8 Schedules and runs to 175 pages. Furthermore, the Act is riddled with references to Regulations. The Secretary of State has made a number of Regulations covering applications for both personal and premises licences and hearings before licensing committees.

Originally responsibility for the legislation was with the DCMS. However, now the Home Office is responsible for the alcohol and late night refreshment aspects of the Act and the DCMS deals with regulated entertainment. Oh what a tangled web!

Licensing objectives

Under-girding the Act, and the way licensing authorities have to carry out their functions under the Act, are four fundamental principles or objectives. These are:

(1) The prevention of crime and disorder.
(2) Public safety.
(3) The prevention of public nuisance.
(4) The protection of children from harm.

Throughout the original Act there were references to actions being "necessary" to the Licensing Objectives. So for example an application could only be refused or conditions imposed if necessary to promote one or more licensing objectives. Following the implementation of the 2011 Act the word "necessary" has been replaced by "appropriate." The word "necessary" means "really needed" or "essential". Changing "necessary" to "appropriate" is a very significant change.

It is clear that whether or not an action is appropriate, e.g. to attach a condition, is a much lower evidential threshold. The word "appropriate" is defined as "right or suitable, fitting". This may lead to a lot of discussion. For example, if the members of a Licensing Sub-Committee decide it is "appropriate" to attach a condition should their decision be accepted and not overturned on appeal? Clearly there must be evidence before the members concerned to justify a condition being attached to an authorisation. It would not appear to be lawful for a condition to be attached to a licence simply because members considered it appropriate to do so when there was no evidence to justify the condition. An example of where a problem may arise is in the case of where the police ask for

CCTV cameras in every licensed premises. Just because the police ask for this condition would it be an "appropriate" condition. On appeal the courts may well ask where is the evidence to justify a requirement that CCTV cameras should be installed in these particular premises.

The statutory guidance under s.182 of the 2003 Act issued by the Home Office in April 2012 has the following thoughts on "appropriate":

Para.9.38—Licensing Authorities are best placed to determine what actions are appropriate for the promotion of the licensing objectives in their area. All licensing determinations should be considered on a case-by-case basis.

Para.9.39—the authority's determination should be evidenced based, justified as being appropriate for the promotion of the licensing objectives and proportionate to what is intended to achieve.

Para.9.40—determination of whether an action or step is appropriate for the promotion of the licensing objectives requires an assessment of what action or step would be suitable to achieve that end. Whilst this does not therefore require a licensing authority to decide that no lesser step will achieve the aim, the authority should aim to consider the potential burden that the condition would impose on the premises licence holder (such as the financial burden due to restrictions on licensable activities) as well as the potential benefit in terms of the promotion of the licensing objectives.

The structure of the Act

Part 1 defines the licensable activities. Essentially, these are:

(1) The retail sale of alcohol.
(2) The supply of alcohol in a club.
(3) The provision of regulated entertainment.
(4) The provision of late night refreshment.

Schedule 1 defines what is meant by "regulated entertainment". Full details are set out in Ch.1 but, in essence, it includes plays, films, indoor sporting events, boxing and wrestling, dancing, live and recorded music and entertainment similar to music and dancing. The entertainment will be regulated if it is provided for members of the public or a section of the public, is provided in qualifying clubs or is provided for profit. The Secretary of State has the power, by Order, to modify the list of regulated activities.

There are a number of exemptions which are detailed in Ch.1; for example, television programmes are exempt, as is any entertainment for the purpose of a religious service or in a building used for public religious worship. Purely incidental recorded music is also not considered to be "regulated entertainment". (This exemption will be extended to live music when the Live Music Act 2012 is brought into force). There are a few exemptions for films, for example those advertising goods or services, or those used as part of an exhibit in a museum. Moving vehicles are also exempt.

Schedule 2 deals with the provision of late night refreshment (defined as the supply of hot food between 11pm and 5am to the public or a section of the public either on or off the premises).

There are a number of exemptions, such as hotels, clubs, vending machines or the supply of hot refreshment by a registered charity.

Again, more comprehensive details are set out in Ch.1.

Part 1 of the Act states the circumstances whereby a licensable activity may take place. Essentially, these are:

- Under the terms of a premises licence.
- Where the activity is a permitted temporary activity.
- When it is a qualifying activity under a club premises certificate.

Chapters 1, 2 and 5 set out these circumstances in more detail.

Part 2 defines the licensing authorities. In London these are the London Boroughs and the Corporation of the City of London. For the rest of England, the licensing authorities will be District Councils or, if there is no District Council, the County Council. In Wales it will be the County Council or County Borough Council as appropriate.

This part of the Act requires the licensing authorities to carry out their functions with a view to promoting the four licensing objectives mentioned earlier. The authority must also have regard to any statutory guidance issued by the Secretary of State and its own licensing statement.

The licensing statement is a policy statement by the authority valid for a three-year period, starting with a date set by the Secretary of State. The date determined by the Secretary of State for the first three-year period was January 7, 2005. Before determining its policy statement, the authority must carry out a consultation exercise involving the police, the fire authority, other responsible authorities and representatives of licensees, club premises, businesses and residents. The policy has to be kept under review. The provisions relating to the making of a policy have been amended by the 2011 Act. As a result of the amendment licensing authorities now have a discretion to review its policy every five years rather than three.

When drafting statements of policies, licensing authorities should have regard to the judgment in the case of *R. (on the application of The British Beer and Pub Association) v Canterbury City Council* [2006] L.G.R. 596. In simple terms, the court made it clear that policies should not be over-prescriptive and suggest requirements that cannot lawfully be imposed on applicants. The court made it clear that it is for applicants to determine the contents of their applications, subject to compliance with the Act and Regulations.

A number of authorities have introduced "cumulative impact policies". There is no mention of such policies in the legislation but reference is made to them in the statutory guidance. The statutory guidance suggests that authorities can introduce "cumulative impact policies". "In some areas, where the number, type and density of premises selling alcohol for consumption on the premises are unusual, serious problems of nuisance and disorder may be arising or have begun to arise outside or some distance from licensed premises." If an application is made for a new licence within the defined area the onus is on the applicant to put forward exceptional reasons as to why the authority should depart from the policy. The decision in *R. (on the application of J D Wetherspoon plc) v Guildford BC* (2006) L.L.R. 312 held that if an application is made to vary an existing premises licence within the defined area the applicant must still put forward exceptional reasons explaining how the increased hours will not add to crime and disorder.

In *R. (on the application of A3D2 Ltd t/a Novus Leisure) v Westminster Magistrates Court* (2011) L.L.R. 303 the court had to consider the situation where the applicant held two premises licences; acquired a third premises licence relating to premises which were being demolished; then applied for a new premises licence incorporating the original two and offered to surrender the third licence. The company argued that the merging of the two licences and surrendering the third amounted to an exceptional circumstance to justify the authority departing from its cumulative impact policy. The High Court held a) the onus fell on the company to persuade the authority to depart from the policy; b) the surrender of the redundant licence could not of itself be capable of rendering the application exceptional in policy terms; c) when premises close because premises are to be demolished the premises licence is effectively a dead premises licence and is of no practical use because the premises to which it relates cannot be used.

Residents put forward an interesting argument considered by a District Judge in *Broad Street Partnership (t/a as Broad Street Business Improvement District) v Birmingham City Council* (Birmingham Magistrates Court October 13, 2010). The application granted by the authority was for a variation of a premises licence to include new rooms so the business could operate as a lap-dancing club. The premises were within the authority's cumulative impact policy area. The residents appealed to the District Judge arguing that the variation of the licence to enable the premises to operate as a lap dancing club would add to cumulative impact in the area. The District Judge held there was no evidence that the variation would add to the cumulative impact relative to alcohol consumption or disorder and therefore the rebuttable presumption not to grant was not triggered.

Each authority has to appoint a licensing committee of between 10 and 15 members who will discharge most of the authority's licensing functions. The licensing committee may establish sub-committees of no more than three members to discharge many of its functions. It is expected that these sub-committees will deal with most individual applications. The Secretary of State has made regulations relating to the proceedings of these sub-committees.

Power is given for decision-making to be delegated to officers; however, there is a list of 15 functions that cannot be delegated. The authority has a duty to keep a register, in a form to be determined by Regulations, and for this register to be kept centrally if desired by the Secretary of State.

Part 3 deals with 'premises licences'. This is a licence that authorises the premises concerned to be used for one or more licensable activities.

It is important to note there are no separate liquor and entertainment licences. The premises licence will cover all licensable activities. Therefore, a public house wanting to provide entertainment can simply add entertainment to the list of activities that are to be included on the premises licence. Similarly, children's certificates were abolished with a presumption that children should be admitted to licensed premises unless there is good reason to exclude them.

Details of who can make an application are detailed in Ch.1. An application has to be accompanied by the fee, a plan and an operating schedule. The application form and detail on the plan and the level of fees are prescribed in the Regulations. If the licensable activities include the sale of alcohol, a person has to be nominated as the 'designated premises supervisor'.

The operating schedule is a document in a form prescribed by the Secretary of State setting out such things as the licensable activities, when they will take place, when the premises will be open to the public, information about the proposed designated premises supervisor and the steps being taken to promote the licensing objectives. The application will have to be publicly advertised in accordance with regulations; these are detailed in Ch.1.

If a valid application is received and no relevant representations are submitted, the authority MUST grant the application. They have no discretion in the matter.

Furthermore, the licence MUST be granted in accordance with the operating schedule subject only to certain mandatory conditions and other conditions consistent with the schedule. Again, there is no discretion for the licensing authority. In *R. (on the application of Bristol City Council) v Bristol Magistrates' Court* (2009) EWCH 625 the High Court held that a) a licensing authority is not tied to the contents of the operating schedule and there is no obligation to attach conditions "consistent with the operating schedule" unless they were necessary and proportionate for the promotion of the licensing objectives and b) that licence conditions must not duplicate other legislation.

If relevant representations are received, a hearing MUST be held unless all parties involved agree that a hearing is unnecessary. If a hearing is held, the authority has more discretion. It can reject the application or grant it. It can exclude certain licensable activities from the licence and can modify the normal conditions to the extent necessary for the promotion of the licensing activities. It can also refuse to specify the nominated person as the designated premises supervisor.

In essence, relevant representations are those relating to the licensing objectives, are made by a responsible authority or other person or a responsible authority within the prescribed time limits and are not vexatious or frivolous. Representations regarding the designated premises supervisor can only be made by the police and, even then, only in exceptional circumstances and where the crime prevention objective would be undermined.

There are certain mandatory conditions and certain prohibited conditions. Equally, there is a host of procedures of which a licensing authority and a licence holder must be aware; these are all detailed in Ch.1.

Part 4 deals with clubs. Basically, the licensing authority can grant a club premises certificate for the supply of alcohol and regulated entertainment to qualifying clubs. These are clubs that are essentially non-profit making clubs. There are various conditions that have to be complied with for a club to qualify and these are detailed in Ch.2.

One major difference between a premises licence and a club premises certificate is in the powers of entry. For a premises licence, entry must be at a reasonable time. For a club premises certificate, it must be at reasonable times, with at least 48 hours' notice and not more than 14 days after the making of an application for the grant or variation of a certificate, or for an application for review. The 14-day period may, in certain circumstances, be extended by a further seven days.

Apart from this, the only power of entry is by a police officer who has reasonable cause to suspect that controlled drugs are being offered or supplied or if there is likely to be a breach of the peace.

Part 5 deals with temporary permitted activities. The first thing to stress is that this is not an occasional licence procedure but a temporarily permitted activity carried on in accordance with a statutory notice.

An individual who wants to use premises for one or more licensable activities in a period not exceeding 168 hours has to give the licensing authority a 'temporary event notice'. The notice has to be in a form prescribed by regulations and must give details of the proposed activities, the times that the activities will take place and whether any sale of alcohol will be made on or off the premises. It also has to state the maximum number of persons permitted on the premises, which must be less than 500 at any one time. There has to be at least 24 hours between the end of one event period and the start of another.

The temporary event notice has to be given in duplicate to the licensing authority, with a copy to the chief officer of police and the Environmental Health Authority, no less than 10 working days before the event period begins. These Authorities then have just three working days to object. The only permitted ground of objection is that the event would undermine one or more of the licensing objectives. Objections are not permitted from any other person or body. "Working day" is any day apart from a weekend on a Bank Holiday.

Full details of temporary event notices are set out in Ch.5.

Part 6 deals with personal licences. A "personal licence" is a licence granted to an individual that will authorise him to supply alcohol or authorise the sale of alcohol in accordance with a premises licence. Such licences are granted for ten-year periods.

The application is made to the licensing authority in whose area the applicant normally lives. If he lives outside England and Wales or has no fixed address, he can choose which authority to apply to. The form of application is, yet again, subject to regulations.

If the applicant meets certain criteria, the authority MUST grant the licence. The criteria are that he must be 18 or over, possesses a licensing qualification, must not have been convicted of relevant or comparable foreign offences and that he has not forfeited a licence in the previous five years. The licensing qualification is one accredited by the Secretary of State or equivalent. Relevant convictions are certain unspent convictions such as sexual and violent offences and offences involving theft, forgery or counterfeiting.

If the applicant is under 18, has no licensing qualification or has forfeited his licence in the previous five years, the authority must reject the application. If he has a relevant conviction, the authority must give notice to the police, who then have 14 days to object if they are satisfied that granting the licence would undermine the crime prevention objective. Full details about personal licences are set out in Ch.3.

If the police object there must be a hearing, unless both parties agree it is unnecessary.

Part 7 deals with offences. There are too many for detailed consideration here but they include unauthorised licensable activities, exposing alcohol for unauthorised sale and keeping alcohol on the premises for unauthorised sale.

There are offences relating to disorderly conduct on licensed premises, the sale of alcohol to drunks or obtaining alcohol for a person who is drunk. Furthermore, a person who is drunk or disorderly commits an offence if he fails to leave the premises when requested by a police officer or by certain other persons, such as the personal licence holder or the designated premises supervisor. There is also an offence relating to the keeping of smuggled goods. A number of offences exist relating to the sale of alcohol to children and provisions relating to test purchases, the confiscation of sealed containers of alcohol, the prohibition of the sale of alcohol on moving vehicles, the power to prohibit the sale of alcohol on trains and false statements.

Part 8 deals with closure orders. Essentially, there are two types of closure order.

The first deals with the closure of licensed premises in a particular area (when it is expected that there will be disorder in that area). A police officer of superintendent rank or above can ask the appropriate Magistrates' Court to order the closure of licensed premises situated at or near the place of disorder or suspected disorder for up to 24 hours. If necessary, the police can use force to implement the closure order.

The second order relates to the closure of identified premises. In this case, a police inspector or higher rank can make a closure order where he reasonably believes that there is, or will imminently be, disorder on the licensed premises or in the vicinity of and related to the premises and, therefore, closure is necessary on public safety grounds. He can also order closure if a public nuisance is caused by noise coming from the premises.

The notice can be served up to 24 hours before the closure and, in certain circumstances, can be extended or cancelled. As soon as possible after a closure order comes into force, the responsible police officer must ask the Magistrates' Court to consider it and any extension. The magistrates may revoke the order or require the premises to be kept closed until certain conditions are met or until the licensing authority has reviewed the premises licence. There is a right of appeal to the Crown Court.

Where a closure order has been made, the licensing authority has 28 days to review the premises licence. When reviewing the licence, the authority may consider any of the licensing objectives. A hearing has to be held and the licence can be modified, revoked or suspended for up to three months.

Part 9 is entitled "Miscellaneous and Supplementary" and is a ragbag of sundry clauses. It covers:

- Relaxation of opening hours for special occasions.
- Various exemptions, for example on an aircraft in flight.
- Certification of premises for national security.
- Exemptions for raffles, etc.
- The prohibition of alcohol sales at service areas, garages, etc.
- Rights of entry.

- Appeals.
- Statutory guidance by the Secretary of State.
- Hearings.
- The giving of notices.
- The provision of information.
- Prosecutions.
- Offences by corporate bodies.
- Vessels, vehicles and movable structures.
- Definitions.
- Regulations and Orders.

Schedule 1 deals with the provision of regulated entertainment and **Schedule 2** with the provision of late night refreshment, both of which were considered earlier.

Schedule 3 lists 28 matters that must be entered in the licensing register.

Schedule 4 lists relevant offences in respect of personal licences.

Schedule 5 sets out details of when an appeal can be lodged to the Magistrates' Court.

Schedules 6 and 7 contain details of minor and consequential amendments and repeals.

Schedule 8 dealt with the transitional arrangements, i.e. the transfer from the previous system to the current regime.

Contents

Table of Cases

Chapter 1

Premises Licences

1.1   Introduction

A **premises licence** is required for licensable activities under the Act. The licensable activities are:

(a)   the sale by retail of alcohol;
(b)   the supply of alcohol by or on behalf of a club to, or to the order of, a member of the club;
(c)   the provision of regulated entertainment (Sch.1); and
(d)   the provision of late night refreshment (Sch.2).

1.2   Sale by retail of alcohol

The term "sale by retail of alcohol" is fairly self-explanatory. It is worth noting, however, that the exemption under the previous legislation of wholesale sales of more than one or two cases (depending on the type of alcohol) has been abolished.

The "sale by retail" of alcohol is a sale to a person other than:

(a)   a trader for trade purposes;
(b)   to a club which holds a club premises certificate;
(c)   to a premises licence holder for purposes permitted by the licence;
(d)   to a personal licence holder for the purposes of making sales authorised by a premises licence;
(e)   to a premises user with a temporary event notice for purposes permitted by the notice.

Thus, "business to business" sales are excluded from the scope of the legislation but other sales are sales by retail and come within the scope of the Act.

1.3   Regulated entertainment

Schedule 1 to the Act sets out the definition of regulated entertainment covered by a premises licence.

Regulated entertainment covers entertainment provided solely or partly for members of the public, or exclusively to club members and their guests, or at other private events for which a charge is made. In other words, it is entertainment provided with a view to profit, a definition which includes raising money for charity. It also covers the provision of facilities for participating in music, dancing or similar entertainment. (It is important to note that the issue is not whether or not a profit was actually made but whether it was intended to make a profit.)

The definition would cover entertainment staged by a charity for the purpose of fundraising, but would not, for example, include the provision of entertainment for a company or firm for its clients, for which no charge was made but which was intended to stimulate general goodwill which might be advantageous for the business.

Forms of entertainment include:

Plays (essentially, a dramatic piece involving the playing of a role and includes rehearsals to which the public are admitted).

The showing of films (defined as any exhibition of moving pictures).

All indoor sporting events. (An indoor sporting event is one which takes place inside a building for spectators wholly inside that building. A sporting event that takes place at a venue whose roof can be opened or closed would not constitute an indoor event, even when the roof is closed. A sporting event is defined as any contest, exhibition or display of any sport in which physical skill is the main factor. For example, tennis would be covered by the definition. However, a game of chess, even if contested publicly, would not.)

Outdoor boxing and wrestling matches. (No other form of outdoor sport is regulated entertainment.)

Music. (Both the public performance of live music and the public playing of recorded music, e.g. as an accompaniment to dancing.)

The public performance of **dance**.

In all cases where the entertainment takes place in the presence of an audience (including spectators).

Entertainment similar to music and/or dancing (e.g. a person gyrating rhythmically).

1.3.1 General exemptions

1.3.1.1 The use of television or radio receivers

The simultaneous reception and playing of a programme included in a programme service within the meaning of the Broadcasting Act 1990; in other words, most radio and television programmes.

1.3.1.2 Religious services, places of worship, etc.

The provision of any entertainment (whether sacred or secular) or of entertainment facilities at a place of public religious worship (but not at ancillary buildings such as a church hall). Consequently, the exemption applies not only to the singing of hymns or other religious material at a religious service, but also to the performance of a classical concert in a church or other building primarily used for religious worship.

The provision of any entertainment or entertainment facilities for the purposes of, or for purposes incidental to, a religious meeting or service. Consequently, for the exemption to apply, the entertainment concerned must either be an integral part of the religious meeting or be purely incidental to that meeting.

The issue will be whether the entertainment is primarily to entertain or whether it is part of a religious meeting. For example, carol singing as part of a carol service would be exempt but carol singing in a shopping mall might well be regarded as a licensable activity if it was an organised event.

1.3.1.3   Garden fêtes, etc.

Entertainment at garden fêtes or similar functions or events, provided that the event concerned is not promoted for the purposes of private gain.

1.3.1.4   Vehicles in motion

Entertainment on vehicles that are in motion and that are not temporarily or permanently parked.

1.3.2   Exemptions for specified types of entertainment

1.3.2.1   Musical entertainment

Music incidental to some other activity, except when that other entertainment is regulated entertainment. For example, background music in a supermarket would be exempt, as would piano music played in the background in a restaurant, but not music being played in the interval of a boxing match.

Music from juke boxes in a public house would be a possible exemption. According to the statutory guidance issued by the Secretary of State, the playing of juke boxes is not a licensable activity as long as the volume of the juke box is not a "high volume". What is "high" is clearly a matter for discussion and possibly determination by the courts in due course.

1.3.2.2   Morris dancing

Morris and similar dancing and any unamplified live music used in connection with such dancing. The 2011 Act has amended this provision to enable amplified music to be played as well as unamplified. There is no definition of what is "similar dancing" to Morris dancing. A common sense view must be that it includes Welsh, Scottish, Irish dancing and any form of cultural dancing.

1.3.2.3 *Sexual entertainment venues*

As a result of an amendment made by the Policing and Crime Act 2009 the provision of relevant entertainment at premises for which a licence for a sexual entertainment venue is required (or the requirement has been waived) is not regarded as regulated entertainment.

1.3.2.4 *Film exhibitions (demonstration, advertisement, education, etc.)*

Film exhibitions where the sole or main purpose of the exhibition is to:

(a)   demonstrate any product;
(b)   advertise any goods or services; or
(c)   provide information, education or instruction.

This would exempt, for example, educational films shown in schools, or special advertisements shown at product display stands in shopping centres.

1.3.2.5 *Museums and art galleries*

Film exhibitions that consist of, or forms part of, an exhibit put on show for any of the purposes of a museum or art gallery.

1.3.3 **Live Music Act 2012**

The 2012 Act will enable premises to have live music without any authorisation provided certain requirements are met. For premises holding a licence authorising the sale of alcohol they will be able to have live music between the hours of 8am and 11pm provided it is unamplified. There will be no limit on the size of the audience. In the case of amplified music the same hours will apply but there is a limit on the size of the audience to 200. For premises not licensed for the sale of alcohol, they will not require a licence for music where it is unamplified and held between 8am and 11pm.

Responsible Authorities and other parties will be able to apply for a review of the premises licence for such licensed premises. At the hearing of the review the licensing authority can remove the right for the premises to have either amplified or unamplified music, or both.

The 2012 Act also exempts live music at unlicensed premises (or licensed only for late night refreshment) at workplaces, (as defined in reg.2(1) of the Workplace (Health, Safety and Welfare) Regulations 1992), provided that the audience does not exceed 200 persons and the performance takes place between 8am and 11pm.

1.4 Late night refreshment

Supply of hot food or drink from premises for consumption on or off those premises between 11pm and 5am. This will include restaurants, take away premises and also burger vans and similar operations that stand outside night clubs in the early hours of the morning. If the street trading legislation is in force in a local authority area and the trader stands on a "street"—as defined in Sch.4 of the Local Government (Miscellaneous Provisions) Act 1982, the London Local Authorities Act 1990 and the City of Westminster Act 1999—they will also require a street trading licence. (*R. (on the application of Kelly) v Liverpool City Council* (2009) L.L.R. 541).

1.4.1 Exemptions

1.4.1.1 Clubs, hotels, etc.

Supply of refreshments to persons solely because they are:

(a) members of a recognised club;

(b) persons staying at a hotel, guest house, hostel, caravan site, camping site or other premises whose primary purpose is the provision of overnight accommodation;
(c) employees of a particular employer;
(d) persons engaged in a particular trade, or who are members of a particular profession or who follow a particular vocation; or
(e) guests of any of the above.

1.4.1.2 *Premises licensed under other legislation*

- Premises licensed for public exhibitions.
- Premises licensed as near beer establishments.

The licensing of public exhibitions only applies to certain named premises in London. Near beer licensing again only applies in London and, in particular, to Westminster and any other London borough that adopts the provisions.

1.4.1.3 *Miscellaneous exemptions*

- The supply of **hot** drink which consists of, or contains, alcohol.
- The supply of **hot** drink by means of a vending machine where a member of the public inserts the payment directly into the machine and the hot drink is supplied directly to that person.
- The supply of hot food or drink free of charge.*
- The supply of hot food or drink by a registered charity or by a person authorised by a registered charity.
- The supply of hot food or drink from a vehicle that is not permanently or temporarily parked.
  *The supply is not regarded as free if, in order to obtain the refreshment, payment has to be made for admission to the premises or for some other item.

1.5 Exemptions from requirement for a licence

Logically, exemptions should have been in one place within the Act. However, tucked away in Pt 9 of the Act are further exemptions which state that no licence is required for a licensable activity if it is carried on:

(a) aboard an aircraft, hovercraft or railway vehicle engaged on a journey;
(b) aboard a vessel engaged on an international journey;
(c) at an approved wharf at a designated port or hoverport;
(d) at an examination station at a designated airport;
(e) at a royal palace;
(f) at premises in respect of which a certificate issued under s.174 (exemption for national security) has effect;
(g) at such other place as may be prescribed (s.173).

Furthermore, the conduct of a lottery, which would require to be licensed by reason of one or more of the prizes consisting of alcohol, is not to be treated as a licensable activity:

(a) if the lottery is promoted as an incident of an exempt entertainment;
(b) if, after deduction of all expenses, the proceeds of the entertainment, including those of the lottery, are applied for purposes other than private gain and the following conditions do not apply:
   (i) the alcohol is not in a sealed container;
   (ii) any prize in the lottery is money;
   (iii) a lottery ticket is sold or issued, or the winners are declared, other than at the premises where the entertainment is taking place and during the entertainment; or
   (iv) the opportunity to participate during the lottery is the only or main inducement to attend the entertainment.

1.6   Restrictions regarding certain 'premises'

1.6.1   *Service areas and garages*

No authorisation under the Act can allow the sale by retail or supply of alcohol on or from a service area on a motorway, or from premises used primarily as a garage. Under previous similar statutory provisions, the courts decided that whether a premises is a garage or not depends on the relative intensity of the use of the premises.

For example, in the case of *R. v Liverpool Crown Court Ex p. Goodwin* (1998) 38 L.R. 21, Laws J. said "The question must be, what is the intensity of use by customers at the premises? So that evidence such as that of customer lists, to take an example, might be highly material." The court held that there had been an "erroneous approach" by the Crown Court in taking the "appearance of the premises and how it is known in the locality" as a factor to determine the nature of the premises. The court indicated that a comparison of "garage use" net turnover, not gross turnover, as compared with the net turnover from other sales is a relevant factor, as is the purposes for which customers visit the garage.

The matter of intensity of use has been considered under the current legislation in *R. (on the application of Murco Petroleum Limited) v Bristol City Council* (2010) EWHC 1992. In that case the Judge held that primary use becomes an issue for a licensing authority where the question of alcohol sales from a garage is raised by a representation. Murco had provided a pie chart showing the percentage of "garage sales" and sales of other items. The Council asked for more information, including turnover figures. The Judge expressed the opinion that "intensity of use" may still be calculated by reference to turnover and that it is a matter for each licensing authority to decide whether to use turnover rather than footfall or customer lists.

9

1.6.2   *Power to prohibit sale of alcohol on trains*

A Magistrates' Court can make an order prohibiting the sale of alcohol on any train or at any specified stations in their area. Such an order can only be made on the application of a senior police officer of or above the rank of inspector (s.157). The Court can only make such an order if it is satisfied that the order is necessary to prevent disorder.

1.7   Who issues the licence?

The authority to issue a premises licence is the authority in which area the premises are situated. In the case of premises which sit in more than one local authority area, the authority in whose area the greater or greatest part of the premises is situated is the licensing authority. If it is not possible to decide in whose area the greater part of the premises is situated, the applicant for the licence must nominate one of the authorities as being the licensing authority (s.12).

1.8   Who can apply for a licence?

The principal category is anyone who carries on, or proposes to carry on, a business involving licensable activities on the premises. This will cover any individual (aged at least 18) or business which wishes to carry on, on a commercial basis, the sale of alcohol, the supply of alcohol by a club, the provision of regulated entertainment or the provision of late night refreshment.

The following may apply for a premises licence:

(1) A person exercising a statutory function (for example, a local authority).
(2) A person exercising any function by virtue of the royal prerogative (for example, a body exercising functions by virtue of a royal charter).
(3) Recognised clubs (see note on Pt 4).

(4) Charities.
(5) Educational institutions.
(6) Health bodies in the public and private sector.
(7) The armed forces.
(8) The police.
(9) Any other category of person prescribed in regulations made by the Secretary of State (s.16).

1.9 How is an application made?

Applications for a premises licence should be made, in the form prescribed in regulations made by the Secretary of State, to the relevant licensing authority, and must be accompanied by:

(a) an operating schedule,
(b) a plan of the premises,
(c) if the application proposes that the licence will authorise the supply of alcohol, a form containing the consent of the individual whom it is proposed will be specified in the licence as the "designated premises supervisor"; and
(d) the appropriate fee (unless exempt).

The operating schedule must set out various details relating to the operation of the premises when carrying on licensable activities, including:

* The licensable activities to be carried out.
* The proposed hours of opening, etc. and the duration of the licence (if it is to have a fixed term).
* Details about the individual (if any) who is to act as the designated premises supervisor.
* Details of whether alcohol is to be supplied (if at all) for on- or off-sales or both.
* A statement of how the applicant intends to promote the licensing objectives (for instance, the arrangements to be put in place to prevent crime and disorder, such as door security).

- Any other information required by regulations made by the Secretary of State.

The significance of the operating schedule is that if the application for the premises licence is approved, it can be incorporated into the licence itself and will set out the permitted activities and the limitations on them. As a consequence, it is the applicant who will decide, subject to the determination of the authority, the nature and the extent of the conditions relating to the carrying on of the activities.

It is important that applicants get this right. If too little information is supplied, the responsible authorities may make representations because they have insufficient information to determine whether the licensing objectives are being sufficiently promoted. On the other hand, if too much information is supplied, the applicant may well find he is bound by a whole host of conditions which limit the flexibility that the Act was designed to achieve. This is because the licensing authority is entitled to convert information in the operating schedule into licence conditions if appropriate to promote the licensing objectives. See the case of *R. (on the application of Bristol City Council) v Bristol Magistrates' Court* (2009) detailed on p.96.

The Regulations require advertising to be done by displaying a notice in at least one place at or on the site of the premises concerned for not less than 28 consecutive days starting on the day following the giving of the application to the licensing authority. The Regulations require the notice to be of at least size A4. The notice must be on pale blue paper and the typeface at least font size 16. The notice must be displayed at a place where it can be conveniently read from the exterior of the premises. In addition, in the case of premises covering an area of more than 50 metres square, a further notice must be displayed every 50 metres along the external perimeter of the premises abutting any highway.

The Regulations also require the applicant to publish a notice on at least one occasion not more than 10 working days after giving the application to the licensing authority (starting on the day following the day on which the application was given) in a local newspaper, newsletter, circular or similar document circulating in the vicinity of the premises.

The information that the premises and newspaper notices must contain includes: the name and postal address of the applicant; the postal address and any website address of the licensing authority; where the register of the relevant licensing authority is kept and where the record of the application may be inspected; the dates within which relevant representations in writing can be made; and a statement of the offence and maximum fine for knowingly or recklessly making a false statement in connection with an application. The notices must also state the relevant licensable or qualifying club activities that it is proposed to carry on; briefly describe the proposed variation in the case of a variation application; and, in the case of a provisional statement application, state that representations are restricted after the issue of a provisional statement.

It should be noted that neither the Act nor the Regulations allow the licensing authority any discretion. So, for example, if the notice was accidentally removed after 14 days, then advertisement of the application will have to start all over again.

Under the 2011 Act the Secretary of State has made regulations putting a requirement on licensing authorities to advertise applications to bring it "to the attention of other persons" i.e. persons who live, or are involved in a business, in the licensing authority area and who are likely to be affected by the application. The regulations require licensing authorities to put details of all applications on their website.

In respect of giving the application to the licensing authority, the word 'given' is defined in the Act as leaving the application with the licensing authority or posting it. It is true that reg.21, relating to premises licences, states that applications can be made electronically provided that certain criteria are met. However, these Regulations also prescribe that when the application has to be accompanied by a fee, plans or other documentation (as will invariably be the case), the application will not be treated as given until the licensing authority receives the fee and plan, etc.

1.10 Determination of application for premises licences

Unless any relevant representations are made to the licensing authority, the application must be granted subject to conditions consistent with those listed by the applicant in the operating schedule and subject to any mandatory conditions (see p.17–20) (s.18). If relevant representations are made, the local authority must hold a hearing. See Ch.7 for details of hearings.

1.11 What are "relevant representations"?

For representations to be relevant they must be made by a responsible authority or other person and must relate to the effect of the grant of the licence on the licensing objectives.

Representations will not be relevant if the licensing authority determines that the representations are irrelevant or, unless they are made by a responsible authority, they are frivolous or vexatious. It is expected that in most cases the decision will be taken by an officer of the licensing authority.

An irrelevant objection is one that does not directly relate to the application and to the promotion of the licensing objectives in the context of the application.

Examples are:

- A representation from a local resident on moral grounds would be irrelevant. A complaint related to general crime and disorder in an area should be deemed irrelevant unless it can be positively linked to the premises in question.

- The term "vexatious" would apply where a licensing authority considers a representation to be based on business rivalry.
- A "frivolous" representation would be one which, having been given due consideration, would be described as 'lacking in seriousness'.

Representations made by a responsible authority cannot be deemed to be frivolous or vexatious.

1.12 Responsible Authorities and other persons

Under the 2003 Act as amended by the 2011 Act "Responsible authority" means any of the following:

- The chief officer of police for any police area in which the premises are situated.
- The fire authority for any area in which the premises are situated.
- The enforcing authority within the meaning given by s.18 of the Health and Safety at Work etc. Act 1974 for any area in which the premises are situated.
- The local planning authority within the meaning given by the Town and Country Planning Act 1990 for any area in which the premises are situated.
- The local authority by which statutory functions are exercisable, in any area in which the premises are situated, in relation to minimising or preventing the risk of pollution of the environment or of harm to human health.
- A body which:
  (a) represents those who, in relation to any such area, are responsible for, or are interested in, matters relating to the protection of children from harm; and
  (b) is recognised by the licensing authority for that area, for the purposes of this section, as being competent to advise it on such matters.
- The weights and measures authority.
- Any licensing authority in whose area part of the premises is situated.

- Primary Care Trusts.
- In relation to a vessel:
  (a) a navigation authority (within the meaning of s.221(1) of the Water Resources Act 1991) having functions in relation to the waters where the vessel is usually moored or berthed or any waters where it is, or is proposed to be, navigated at a time when it is used for licensable activities;
  (b) the Environment Agency;
  (c) the British Waterways Board; or
  (d) the Secretary of State.

The 2003 Act restricted the ability to make representations to responsible authorities and interested parties—essentially people who loved and worked in the vicinity of the premises concerned. The 2011 Act removed both the terms "interested parties" and "vicinity of the premises." In theory, therefore, a person living in London could object to an application for a premises licence in Leeds. However, the amended Act refers to advertising an application to bring it to the attention of persons likely to be affected by the application. If, as in this example, a person is highly unlikely to be affected by the application the relevant licensing authority would be entitled to regard the representation as irrelevant and/or vexatious.

1.13 Mandatory conditions

The mandatory conditions that must be attached to licences authorising the sale of alcohol are:

(a) that, at any time when sales of alcohol are made, there must be a designated premises supervisor who is the holder of a valid personal licence; and
(b) every sale of alcohol must be made or authorised by a personal licence holder. In other words, sales must be made personally by a personal licence holder or by an individual authorised by a personal licence holder. It is not necessary for either the designated premises supervisor or a personal licence holder to be present when alcohol is

sold (see below). Nevertheless, a personal licence holder who has authorised a person to sell alcohol is still responsible for such sale even if he is not personally present.

1.13.1 Authorisation

The term "authorise" has caused considerable confusion. It is clear from the Act that Parliament did not intend each and every sale to be authorised by a personal licence holder. This is because the wording in s.19(3), that every sale of alcohol must be made or authorised by a personal licence holder, is very different from that used in s.153 (prohibition of unsupervised sales by children) which refers to a sale or supply of alcohol being "specifically approved". This view is supported by the statutory guidance.

Indeed, the statutory guidance makes it quite clear that a personal licence holder can be absent from the premises for periods when alcohol is being sold. However, there will obviously come a point where the frequency or length of absence means that the personal licence holder could not have authorised the sale. There seems little doubt that this issue will ultimately be determined by the courts on the facts of particular cases.

In the meantime, the Department for Culture, Media and Sport (DCMS) have stated that it "seems reasonable to expect that the courts would require the authorisation to be meaningful and not simply an abdication of responsibility".

The current DCMS Guidance indicates the "following factors might be relevant in considering whether or not an authorisation has been given":

- The person(s) authorised to sell alcohol should be clearly identified.
- The authorisation should have specified the acts that may be carried out by the person being authorised.

- There should be an overt act of authorisation; for example, a specific written statement given to the individual who is authorised to sell alcohol;and individual(s) being authorised.
- There should be in place sensible arrangements for the monitoring by the personal licence holder of the activity authorised by him on a reasonably regular basis.

Whilst it is perfectly legal for an authorisation to be in oral form, the authors consider that to avoid any possible misunderstanding it would be sensible for the authorisation to be in written form. This could well avoid disputes at a later stage if problems arose.

As the personal licence holder is to a large extent responsible for the actions of the person being authorised to sell alcohol, he would be advised to ensure that the person being authorised fully understands his legal responsibilities and acknowledges this fact in writing. In many cases, it might be appropriate to ensure the person being authorised has been properly trained and holds an appropriate qualification such as the BIIAB Award in Responsible Alcohol Retailing.

1.13.2   Further mandatory conditions

Where a licence is issued with a condition that at specified times one or more persons must be at the premises to carry out a security activity (usually door supervisors), a condition must be attached to the licence that all such persons must be licensed by the Security Industry Authority (s.19). This would apply irrespective of whether the condition was imposed at a licensing hearing or offered by the applicant in his operating schedule.

Where a premises licence authorises the showing of films, a condition must be attached restricting the admission of children to such films, either in accordance with council requirements or with a film classification body (s.20). It should be noted that the Act brought to an end the classification of films to be shown to adults by means of licence conditions.

Conversely, a licensing authority is prohibited from attaching a condition relating to the nature of a play, except a condition made on safety grounds (s.22).

Schedule 4 of the Policing and Crime Act 2009 amended the Licensing Act 2003 and introduced additional mandatory conditions which now apply to all premises licences authorising the sale or supply of alcohol. These conditions are:

(a) The responsible person must take all reasonable steps to ensure that staff on licensed premises do not carry out, arrange or participate in any irresponsible promotions relating to the premises.

(b) Irresponsible promotions means any one or more of the following activities, or substantially similar activities that are carried on in such a way that there is significant risk of the premises being in breach of any of the licensing objectives:

- Games which require or encourage people to drink a quantity of alcohol within a time limit (other than to consume drinks already purchased before the premises closes), or to drink as much alcohol as possible, even without a time limit.
- Unlimited or unspecified amounts of alcohol being given free or for a fixed fee to the public or a group defined by a particular characteristic, i.e. all you can drink for £10; women drink free; student discount nights etc. (does not apply if offer is linked to the consumption of a table meal).
- Free or discounted alcohol (or anything else, such as free concert tickets) as a prize to encourage or reward the purchase and consumption of alcohol over a 24 hour period, or less.
- Free or discounted alcohol linked to a sporting event, such as free drinks for 30 minutes after the game if a certain team wins, or greatly reduced shots every time a try is scored.
- Selling or supplying alcohol in association with promotional posters or flyers which condone or glamorise anti-social behaviour.

19

- "Dentist chair" games where alcohol is dispensed by one person directly into the mouth of another. This does not apply if the person receiving the drink cannot do so otherwise due to disability.

(c) Free tap water is to be provided to customers on request where it is reasonably available.

(d) Each premises has to have an age verification policy in place, requiring all staff to check the identity of anyone appearing to be under the age of 18years (or any such older age as may be specified in the policy).

(e) Smaller measures of the following must be available, and customers made aware of their availability:
- Beer or cider: ½ pint.
- Gin, rum, vodka or whisky: 25 ml or 35 ml.
- Wine by the glass (still): 125 ml.

1.13.3 Representations regarding the designated premises supervisor

Only the police can object to a person being named in a licence as the "Designated Premises Supervisor"; they can only object to this person in exceptional circumstances and on the grounds that they consider the designation of the person as a premises supervisor would undermine the crime prevention objective.

1.14 Special provisions relating to dancing and music in certain small premises (section 177)

Parliament inserted special provisions into the Act that were designed to encourage live music in licensed premises, by attempting to ensure that operators are not subject to what were claimed to be unnecessary conditions on the premises licence (or a club premises certificate) where such entertainment takes place.

Essentially, this section makes special provisions where:

(a) a premises licence (or club premises certificate) authorises the sale of alcohol on the premises and the provision of music entertainment (live music or dancing);
(b) the relevant premises are used primarily for the consumption of alcohol on the premises (e.g. a public house); and
(c) the premises has a capacity limit of up to 200 persons.

Any conditions relating to the provision of the music entertainment imposed by the licensing authority will be suspended unless imposed on grounds of public safety or the prevention of crime and disorder.

The suspension does not apply to conditions offered by the licence holder in the operating schedule.

In addition, where a premises licence or club premises certificate authorises the provision of music entertainment and the premises have a capacity limit of 200 people or less, then between 8am and midnight, if the premises are used for live unamplified music (but no other form of regulated entertainment), **any** condition imposed by the licensing authority in relation to the provision of the music entertainment will be suspended. Again, the suspension does not apply to conditions offered by the licence holder in the operating schedule.

Finally, in both cases, these suspension provisions can be disapplied in relation to particular conditions on review of the premises licence or club premises certificate.

It is important to note that only conditions that are imposed are suspended, where this concession is used, so the licensing authority and the licence holder will need to be clear which conditions were voluntarily agreed and will be in force and which were imposed and therefore suspended.

The Live Music Act 2012 when it comes into force will amend s.77 (see pp.5–6 for details).

1.15   Notification of grant of a premises licence

If the council grants a premises licence, they must forthwith inform the applicant, any person who made relevant representations in respect of the application and the police of the fact that the licence has been granted. They must also forthwith issue the applicant with the licence and a summary of it (s.23).

Should an application be refused, the council must forthwith inform the applicant, any person who made representations in respect of the application and the police of the decision giving reasons for the decision made (s.23(3)).

1.16   How long does a licence last?

Unless a licence is transferred, surrendered or revoked, it will last for as long as the licensee continues to operate the business. There is one exception which is where application is made for a premises licence for a specified period of time. Here, the licence will expire at the end of the time specified (s.26). An example of this would be festivals such as Glastonbury and Reading where temporary event notices could not be used because of the size of the event (accommodation well in excess of 499) and a permanent licence would not be appropriate.

It is important for licensing authorities to appreciate that they have no power to time limit a premises licence. For a licence to be granted other than on a permanent basis, the applicant must ask for this in the application.

1.17   Surrender of a licence

The holder of the licence can surrender it by giving notice to the licensing authority. The notice must be accompanied by the licence or, if that is not possible, a statement setting out why it is not practicable to attach the licence. The premises licence will lapse on receipt of the notice by the authority (s.28).

1.18   Loss, etc. of a premises licence

If a premises licence is lost, stolen, damaged or destroyed, the holder can apply to the licensing authority for a copy of the licence (s.25). The licensing authority must issue the holder of a licence with a copy of it if they are satisfied the licence has been lost, stolen, damaged or destroyed and, where it has been lost or stolen, the matter has been reported to the police.

1.19   Change of address of a premises licence holder or designated premises supervisor

Should the holder of a premises licence change their name or address, they must inform the licensing authority of this as soon as practicable. There is also a responsibility on the holder of the premises licence to inform the licensing authority of a change of the name or address of the designated premises supervisor, unless that person has already done so (s.33).

1.20   Variations of a premises licence

The holder of a premises licence can apply to vary the licence to include a new activity or extend the licensing hours, or to vary substantially the premises to which the licence relates. The application must be advertised in the same way as a new application. If no relevant representations are made the variation must be granted. If relevant representations are made, the licensing authority must arrange a hearing, unless it decides that representations made by other persons are frivolous or vexatious or everyone involved with the matter agrees that the need for a hearing can be dispensed with (ss.34 and 35).

If relevant representations are made, the licensing authority must, if it is considered appropriate for the promotion of the licensing objectives, modify the conditions of the licence or reject the application for variation on whole or in part. A licensing authority, when varying a premises licence, can impose different conditions on different parts of the premises, or impose different conditions in relation to different licensable activities.

The authority must notify its decision to the applicant, police and any person who has made relevant representations and must give reasons for its decision.

1.20.1 Variations—supply of alcohol from community premises.

Where a management committee holds a premises licence in respect of community premises it can apply to vary the licence so as to replace two mandatory conditions with an alternative licence condition. The conditions to be replaced are those requiring the premises to have a designated premises supervisor and for every sale of alcohol to be made or authorised by a personal licence holder. The alternative licence condition would require every supply of alcohol under the premises licence to be made or authorised by the management committee.

The chief officer of police is the only person who can object to such an application and only on the basis that in the exceptional circumstances of the case he is satisfied that granting the application would undermine the crime prevention objective.

1.20.2 Minor variations

The Licensing Act 2003 (Premises Licences & Club Premises Certificate) (Miscellaneous Amendments) Regulations 2009 introduced minor variations. There is no definition of what constitutes a "minor variation" although the Act prohibits certain applications from being the subject of a minor variation procedure e.g. adding alcohol as an authorised activity. The procedure could be used to reduce the hours for the sale of alcohol; ask for unnecessary conditions to be removed from the licence or certificate. A minor variation cannot be used to:

(1) Transfer a licence or certificate.
(2) Specify in a premises licence a new Premises Supervisor.
(3) Add the sale by retail or supply of alcohol at any time between 11pm and 7am.
(4) Authorise an increase in the amount of time on any day during which alcohol may be sold by retail or supplied.

The power to make a decision on whether or not to approve an application for a minor variation lies with the Licensing Officer. The officer should consider whether the variation will adversely affect any of the Licensing Objectives. If it could the application must be refused. There is no right of appeal against a decision by the officer to refuse an application; the only challenge is by way of Judicial Review. If an application is refused the fee must be returned.

An application for a minor variation must be made on the prescribed form; submitted to the Licensing Authority; advertised on or near the premises concerned for 10 working days by means of a white notice. The Licensing Authority may consult such of the Responsible Authorities as they consider appropriate but must make a decision on the application within 15 working days of its receipt. If no decision is made by this time the application is deemed to be rejected and the fee must be returned. However, the applicant can agree with the authority that the time for consideration of the application can start again.

1.21   Designated premises supervisor

1.21.1   *Changes of supervisor*

In addition to varying the actual licence, the holder of a premises licence can apply to substitute a different person for the designated premises supervisor. The application must be accompanied by the premises licence as well as a form of consent signed by the proposed premises supervisor. The applicant must also notify the police and the existing designated supervisor of the application.

Only the police can object to the naming of a new designated premises supervisor, and only if they consider it would undermine the crime prevention objective.

The authority must notify the applicant, the police and the proposed premises supervisor of its decision, giving reasons. If the application is to vary the designated premises supervisor, the licence holder must notify the person, if any, who is being replaced as such supervisor (ss.39 to 40).

An application to vary a premises licence, so as to name a new designated premises supervisor, can be given immediate effect if the premises licence holder requests this at the time the application is made. This enables the supply of alcohol to continue at the premises if the existing premises supervisor is suddenly unable to carry out their duties.

1.21.2 Request to be removed as a designated premises supervisor

A designated premises supervisor who wishes to stop acting in that capacity can give notice to the local authority. If that person is also the premises licence holder, the notice must be accompanied by the premises licence or an explanation as to why it is not attached.

If the designated premises supervisor is not the premises licence holder then, in addition to giving notice to the licensing authority within 48 hours, a copy of the notice must be supplied to the premises licence holder with a direction that, within 14 days, the premises licence must be sent to the licensing authority or, if this not possible, an explanation as to why it has not been done (s.41).

1.22 Provisional statement

In relation to premises which are being (or are about to be) constructed, extended or altered for use for licensable activities, a person interested in the premises may apply to the licensing authority for a 'provisional statement'. The idea behind the provision is to establish a mechanism to enable people who are about to construct or develop premises to be used for licensable activities, or substantially alter premises already licensed, to obtain an indication of the likely effect of the intended licensable activities on the licensing objectives and of the prospects of any future application for a premises licence (s.29).

An application for a provisional statement must be advertised in the same way as for a premises licence (s.30). If no relevant representations are made, the licensing authority must issue a provisional statement in accordance with the application, stating that no relevant representations have been made.

However, if relevant representations are made, a hearing must take place—unless they are made by a person other than a responsible authority and the council decides that they are frivolous or vexatious. If a hearing is held, the licensing authority must decide if the premises were constructed or altered in the way proposed and, if a premises licence was sought for the premises, whether it would consider it appropriate for the promotion of the licensing objectives to attach conditions to the licence, to rule out any of the licensable activities applied for, to refuse to accept the person specified as the designated premises supervisor or to reject the application (s.31).

It is important to note that a licensing authority cannot reject an application for a provisional statement. A valid application must always be granted. However, as set out above, the licensing authority can indicate in the statement that if an application was made for a premises licence in similar terms, it would be likely to be rejected.

Where a premises licence is later sought for premises in respect of which a provisional statement has been issued, responsible authorities and other persons will, provided that the application is in the same form as that made for the provisional statement, not be able to make representations on such

27

applications in respect of matters upon which representations could have been made by them when the provisional statement was applied for.

However, this does not apply if a person who wishes to make representations has a reasonable excuse for not having made those representations at the time the application for the provisional statement was considered, or if they has been a material change in the circumstances relating to those premises or to the area in the vicinity of those premises since that time (s.32).

1.23 Things that can happen during the currency of a licence

1.23.1 Death, etc. of the premises licence holder

A premises licence will lapse if the holder dies or becomes mentally incapable or insolvent, in the case of a company if it is dissolved or, in the case of a club, if it ceases to be a recognised club.

In the initial twenty-eight days after the lapse of a premises licence due to the death, mental incapacity or insolvency of a premises licence holder, those with a prescribed interest in the relevant premises or those connected to the licence holder (by virtue of being the licence holder's personal representative, having an enduring or lasting power of attorney in respect of the individual, acting as the insolvency practitioner or having registered an interest in the premises), can give an interim authority notice to the relevant licensing authority. However, no notice can be given if an application for a transfer of the premises licence has already been made. A copy of the interim authority notice must also be given to the chief officer of police by the end of the initial seven-day period. The effect of such a notice will be to reinstate the lapsed premises licence and for the person who gave that notice to become the licence holder, from the time the authority receives the notice for two months, or until terminated by the person who gave notice, unless a successful transfer application is made to the relevant authority within that time. The reinstated licence will also lapse if the police are not notified of the giving of the notice within the initial twenty-eight day period.

The police can object within 48 hours of being notified of an interim authority notice, but they can do so only when they believe that exceptional circumstances mean that a failure to cancel the notice would undermine the crime prevention objective. In such cases, the authority must hold a hearing to decide whether or not to cancel the notice. The need for a hearing can be dispensed with by agreement of the authority, the police and the person who has given the interim authority notice. If the authority considers it necessary for the promotion of the crime prevention objective, it must cancel the interim authority notice. If it does so, the licence will lapse. A cancellation must be notified to the police and to the person who gave the interim authority notice (ss.47 and 48).

1.23.2 *Transfer of licences*

People or bodies who may apply for the transfer of a premises licence are the same as the people and bodies who may apply to be granted a premises licence under s.17. Any such application must be in a form prescribed by the Secretary of State and accompanied by a fee. The application must also be accompanied by the premises licence (unless that is impracticable and then the applicant must state the reasons why this is the case). The applicant must notify the chief officer of police for the area of the application. The police can object to the transfer if they believe there are exceptional circumstances whereby the grant of the application would undermine the crime prevention objective and, if so, they must notify the licensing authority and provide reasons for the objection within 14 days.

A person applying for the transfer of a premises licence may request that it be given immediate effect. Such an application generally requires the consent of the holder of the premises licence. No consent is required if the applicant can show that he has taken all reasonable steps to obtain that consent and that he is in a position to use the premises straightaway for the licensable activities authorised by the licence.

Where a person applies for a premises licence to be transferred to him, s.44 provides that the licensing authority must reject the application unless:

(i)   the transfer application has been given immediate effect;
(ii)   the existing licence holder has agreed to the transfer; or
(iii) the applicant has been exempted from the need to obtain that consent.

An applicant will be exempted if he can show that he has taken all reasonable steps to obtain that consent, and that he is in a position to use the premises straightaway for the licensable activities authorised by the licence.

If the police have notified the licensing authority of objections, the authority must hold a hearing to consider the application for transfer and, if it considers it appropriate for the promotion of the crime prevention objection, must reject the application. The need for a hearing can be dispensed with by agreement of the authority, the applicant for the transfer and the police.

An applicant for the transfer of a premises licence must notify the designated premises supervisor specified in that licence of his application and, if the application is successful, of the transfer of the premises licence to him (s.46). Obviously, this section does not apply where the applicant for transfer is the designated premises supervisor.

Where a premises licence lapses (death, incapacity or insolvency of the holder, etc.), or if it is surrendered but no interim authority notice has effect, a person who may apply for the grant of a premises licence may apply within seven days of the lapse for the transfer of the licence to him. This will cause the licence to be reinstated from the point at which the transfer application is received by the licensing authority. Only one such transfer application can be made in these circumstances (s.50(7)).

1.24 Review of premises licence

The fact that there is no renewal procedure for premises licences is designed to ensure that responsible operators who comply with the licensing objectives can operate with a minimum of interference. However, the Act provides for the licences of premises causing problems to be reviewed and, if necessary, revoked, suspended or amended. The basic procedure is as follows:

- An applicant seeking a review must give written notice of the application to the licensing authority, and on the same day give a copy to the premises licence holder, or club premises certificate holder, and to each responsible authority.
- The authority must reject an application unless it is relevant to at least one of the licensing objectives, or if the application is made by by a person other than a responsible authority, if it is:
  (a) frivolous;
  (b) vexatious; or
  (c) repetitious (namely, identical or substantially similar to a ground for review already considered by the authority in a previous review, or in the determination of the application for grant of the licence, and a reasonable period has not passed since the time—the statutory guidance suggests 12 months would normally be a reasonable period of time, other than in compelling circumstances).
- An applicant seeking a review must give written notice of the application to the licensing authority and, on the same day, give a copy to the premises licence holder or club premises certificate holder and to each responsible authority.

- The licensing authority must advertise the application and invite representations from responsible authorities and other persons. The application must be advertised by displaying a notice in the form prescribed by the Regulations (at least A4 in size, pale blue in colour and in black type of at least font size 16) for not less than 28 consecutive days, commencing on the day after the application was received by the authority for all review applications other than those relating to closure orders, where the notice need only be displayed for five days. The notice has to be displayed at or near the site of the premises concerned where it can be read by the public. Where the premises covers an area of more than 50 square metres, further notices in the form outlined above must be displayed every 50 metres along any external boundary of the premises adjacent to the highway. If the authority concerned has a website, it must also publish a notice on that website. The notice advertising the review must contain the following information:
  - (a) the address of the premises for which a review application has been received;
  - (b) the dates between which representations may be made by responsible authorities and other persons;
  - (c) the grounds on which the application for review has been made;
  - (d) the postal address and, where relevant, the website address where the register of the relevant licensing authority is kept, and details of when and where the grounds for review may be inspected; and
  - (e) a statement that it is an offence to knowingly or recklessly make a false statement in connection with an application and details of the maximum fine payable on conviction of such an offence.
- The licensing authority must then arrange a hearing at which all parties may put their case.
- At such a hearing the authority may take any of the following steps that they consider to be appropriate to promote the licensing objectives. They may:
  - (a) modify the conditions of the licence;

(b) exclude a licensable activity from the scope of the licence;

(c) remove the designated premises supervisor (where premises licence authorises sale of alcohol);

(d) suspend the licence for a period not exceeding three months;

(e) revoke the licence.

"Modification" of the conditions of a licence includes adding new conditions as well as altering or omitting any existing conditions.

Where conditions are modified, or where a licensable activity is excluded, the authority can, if it wishes, limit the changes to a period not exceeding three months.

The licensing authority may, of course, decide to take none of these steps and leave the licence untouched.

• The licensing authority must notify all parties of its determination and provide reasons for its decision. Any party to the hearing may appeal against a decision of the authority by giving notice to the Magistrates' Court within 21 days of being notified of the decision.

• A review decision does not have effect until the time for bringing an appeal has expired and, if an appeal is lodged, until the determination or withdrawal of the appeal.

When considering a case regarding conditions imposed on a premises licence at the end of a second review for underage sales of alcohol the High Court made the following observation "On a second review (for underage sales of alcohol) rather than start with a consideration of the evidence and what was proportionate for the promotion of the licensing objectives there would be a presumption of revocation. It would be of no consequence that the revocation was not imposed but that revocation was the starting point." (*R. (on the application of Somerfield Stores Ltd) v Hinckley Magistrates Court & Blaby DC* (2011) L.L.R. 669).

1.24.1 *Summary review*

Section 21 of the Violent Crime Reduction Act 2006 inserted a s.53(A1) into the 2003 Act. This introduced a power for the police to ask for a summary review of a premises licence which authorises the sale of alcohol. The procedure for such a review is that senior police officer (an officer of the rank of Superintendent or above) must complete a certificate that, in their opinion, the premises are associated with serious crime or serious disorder or both. The chief officer of police may then apply to the licensing authority for a review of the premises licence. The certificate provided by the senior officer must accompany the application.

The licensing authority must advertise the application for a summary review for a period of seven days between the first working day after the day on which the application was received and the date of the ninth subsequent working day.

When the licensing authority receives an application for a summary review within 48 hours of receipt consideration must be given whether any interim steps are necessary pending the final decision. In calculating the 48 hour period any day that is not a working day (weekend or Bank Holiday) is not taken into account.

The decision whether or not to take interim steps must be taken by the Licensing Committee or Sub-Committee. The interim steps that the authority must consider taking are:

(a) Modification of the conditions of the premises licence.
(b) The exclusion of the sale of alcohol by retail.
(c) The removal of the designated premises supervisor.
(d) The suspension of the licence.

There is no need for the holder of the premises licence to attend the hearing where interim steps are considered but statutory guidance suggests they should be invited if it is possible to do so.

If interim steps are taken they have immediate effect and the authority must immediately notify the premises licence holder and the police. Reasons must be given for the decision. If the holder of the licence makes representations about the steps the authority must hold a hearing within 48 hours to consider them. The licence holder and the police must be given notice of this hearing. There is no time limit for the licence holder to make representations to the interim steps.

At the hearing the authority has to consider whether the interim steps imposed are appropriate to promote the licensing objectives and then decide whether or not to modify or withdraw any of them. The members must consider the certificate submitted by the police, any representations made by the police and the representations made by the licence holder.

The final hearing of the summary review application must be made within 28 days of the application being received by the authority. The Licensing Act 2003 (Hearings) Regulations 2005 apply to the final hearing so five days notice must be given.

The steps that can be taken at the final hearing are:

(a) The modification of the conditions on the licence—this includes the alteration or removal of existing conditions or the addition of new ones.
(b) The exclusion of licensable activities.
(c) The removal of the designated premises supervisor.
(d) The suspension of a licence for a period not exceeding three months.
(e) The revocation of the licence.

There has been some discussion about how long the interim steps stay in force. Do they end when the final hearing has taken place? If the premises licence holder appeals against the final decision do the interim steps stay in force pending the determination of the appeal? In a Magistrates Court decision the District Judge held that the steps came to an end when the final hearing took place and if the licence holder appealed

35

against the final decision the interim steps did not remain in force. (*Chief Constable of Cheshire v Oates* (December 19, 2011)).

1.24.2 Fees

The licence holder is required to pay an annual fee to the Licensing Authority and the original Act simply stated that any fee owed to the Licensing Authority may be recovered as a debt to the authority. An amendment made by the 2011 Act will require the Licensing Authority to suspend the premises licence if the fee is not paid by the end of the "grace period" of 21 days after it became due.

The Authority is required to give at least two working days notice of suspension to the licence holder. (The statutory guidance encourages longer notice). The suspension ends when the fee is paid and the Licensing Authority must give the holder written acknowledgement as soon as practicable.

1.25 Looking after the licence

The holder of a premises licence must ensure that the original document, or a certified copy of it, is held on the premises to which it relates, either by the licence holder or a person nominated by the licence holder. A summary of the licence and a notice stating the name of the individual responsible for custody of the licence, if not the licence holder, must be displayed prominently on the premises (s.57).

A copy of a premises licence, or summary of it, is to be certified as a true copy by the licensing authority, a solicitor or notary, or other person prescribed by the Secretary of State (s.58).

1.26   Inspection of premises

1.26.1   *Before a licence is granted or on review*

A police constable or an authorised officer of the licensing or fire authority may, at any reasonable time, enter a premises to which an application relates before it has been determined. If an application is made for a review of a licence, a police officer or an authorised officer can enter the premises using reasonable force if necessary (s.59).

1.26.2   *Right of entry to inspect licensable activities*

- A police officer or authorised person may, at any time, enter any premises if they have reason to believe that the premises are being used, or are about to be used, for a licensable activity (s.179).
- Such checks would be carried out to check whether the activity is licensed or is being carried out in accordance with the conditions of the licence.

1.26.3   *Right of entry to investigate offences*

A police officer may enter and search any premises at any time if he has reason to believe that an offence under the Licensing Act has been, is being, or is about to be committed. No search warrant is required (s.180).

1.26.4   *Offences of obstruction*

- Reasonable force may be used by a police officer or authorised person, if necessary, in order to exercise the above powers.
- Section 179 makes it an offence to obstruct an authorised person in the exercise of these powers and it is a criminal offence under the Police Act 1996 to obstruct a police officer in the execution of his duty.

An authorised person includes:

(a) an officer of the licensing authority authorised by the authority;
(b) an inspector appointed under the Fire Precautions Act 1971;
(c) an inspector appointed under the Health and Safety at Work etc Act 1974;
(d) an officer of a local authority for the area where the premises are situated, authorised by the authority under legislation relating to the risk of pollution of the environment or of harm to health, e.g. Environmental Protection Act 1990.

Chapter 2

Club Premises Certificates

2.1 Introduction

A **club premises certificate** enables qualifying clubs meeting specified criteria to carry on licensable activities at their premises.

Qualifying club activities are:

(1) The supply of alcohol by clubs to members for consumption on the premises.
(2) The sale by retail of alcohol by clubs to members' guests for consumption on the premises.
(3) The provision of regulated entertainment by the club for its members and guests.

In respect of a club holding a club premises certificate, there is no need for there to be a holder of a personal licence or a designated premises supervisor for the sale of alcohol to take place.

The general conditions for a club to be a qualifying club are as follows:

- Nobody can be admitted as a member without an interval of at least two days between their nomination or application for membership and their admission.
- A person who is admitted as a member other than by prior nomination or application must wait at least two days before enjoying the privileges of membership.
- The club must be established and conducted in good faith as a club.
- The club must have at least 25 members.

- No alcohol is supplied, or is intended to be supplied, on the club premises except by and on behalf of the club (s.62).

Section 63 of the Act provides that, in determining whether or not a club is established and conducted in good faith, the matters to be taken into account are:

(1) The club's freedom to purchase alcohol.
(2) How money or property belonging to the club is used.
(3) Arrangements for giving members information about the finances of the club.
(4) The club's accounts.
(5) The nature of the premises occupied by the club.

There are three additional conditions a club must satisfy if it is to be a qualifying club in relation to the supply of alcohol to members. The conditions are that:

(a) the purchase and supply of alcohol should be managed by a committee consisting of members of the club, who are over 18 years of age and elected by members of the club;
(b) nobody can receive, at the expense of the club, a commission or percentage deriving from the purchase of alcohol; and
(c) nobody should receive a pecuniary benefit from the supply of alcohol by the club to its guests (s.64).

2.2 The application

The application is made to the licensing authority by submitting:

(a) the application form;
(b) the appropriate fee;
(c) a club operating schedule;
(d) a plan of the premises to which the application relates, in the prescribed form; and

40

(e)   a copy of the club's rules.

The operating schedule will set out:

(a)   the qualifying club activities to be carried out;
(b)   the proposed hours of those activities and other times when it is proposed that the premises will be open to members and their guests; and
(c)   a statement of how it is intended that the licensing objectives will be promoted.

The significance of the operating schedule is that, if the application for the club premises certificate is granted, the details will be incorporated into the certificate.

If no relevant representations are made in respect of an application for a club premises certificate then the application must be granted.

Section 72 provides that, where relevant representations are made by a responsible authority or other person and a hearing does take place, the licensing authority must, if it considers it appropriate for the promotion of the licensing objectives:

(a)   attach conditions to any certificate granted;
(b)   exclude from the certificate any of the qualifying club activities applied for; or
(c)   reject the application.

The licensing authority can impose different conditions on different parts of the premises, or impose different conditions in relation to different qualifying club activities.

Subject to conditions, a club premises certificate can authorise the supply of alcohol for consumption off the premises, provided that it also authorises the supply of alcohol to a member of a club for consumption on the premises. The conditions allowing sales of alcohol for consumption off the premises are:

(a) the supply must be made at a time when the premises are open for the purpose of supplying alcohol to members;
(b) any alcohol must be in a sealed container;
(c) any supply of alcohol for consumption off the premises must be made to a member of the club in person.

Where a licensing authority makes a decision in respect of an application for club premises certificate, they must inform the applicant, any person who made relevant representations and the police of their decision. This must be done forthwith.

2.3 Theft or loss of a certificate

If a club premises certificate or summary of it is lost, stolen, damaged or destroyed, an application can be made to the licensing authority for a copy. If the licensing authority is satisfied that the certificate or summary has been lost, stolen, damaged or destroyed and, where it has been lost or stolen, the matter has been reported to the police, the licensing authority must issue the club with a copy of the certificate.

2.4 Change of name, rules or address

If there is any change in the name or the rules of the club, the secretary must inform the licensing authority and the club premises certificate must be amended to record any such change. It is an offence not to notify the authority of any such change within 28 days (s.82). If there is any change to the club's address, they may notify the licensing authority of this, but the club must notify the licensing authority if its ceases to make use of the address which it has given as its relevant registered address. It is an offence not to do so (s.83).

2.5 Variation of a certificate

A club can apply, in the prescribed form, to vary its club premises certificate in any way other than to vary substantially the premises to which the certificate relates (ss.84 and 86).

Unless a responsible authority or other person makes relevant representations, the licensing authority must grant the application. Where relevant representations are made to the licensing authority and are not withdrawn and, in the case of relevant representations by a person other than a responsible authority, they are not frivolous or vexatious in the opinion of the licensing authority, the licensing authority must hold a hearing (s.85).

Having considered the representations, the council must (if they believe it is appropriate for the promotion of the licensing objectives):

(a)   modify the conditions of the certificate; or
(b)   reject the whole or part of the application.

Modification of conditions includes adding completely new conditions as well as altering or omitting existing conditions.

The licensing authority must inform the applicant, anyone who made a relevant representation and the police of the licensing authority's decision forthwith, giving reasons for the decision.

When making a decision concerning an application for a variation of a club premises certificate, the licensing authority can vary the certificate so that different conditions apply to different parts of the premises and to different club activities.

The procedure for a minor variation is available for the holders of Club Premises Certificates (see Ch.1 on premises licences).

2.6 Review of a club premises certificate

A responsible authority or other person can apply to the licensing authority for a review of the club premises certificate (s.87).

The licensing authority can reject any ground for a review if they are satisfied it is not relevant to one or more of the licensing objectives or, if made by a person other than a responsible authority, it is frivolous or vexatious or is a repetition (s.87(4)).

A ground is a repetition if it is identical, or substantially similar, to a ground for review mentioned in an earlier application for a review in respect of the same club premises certificate, or identical or substantially similar to representations considered by the licensing authority when determining the application for the club premises certificate.

Section 87(4) provides that, when dealing with an application for review of a club premises certificate, and relevant representations have been made, the licensing authority must (if it considers it appropriate for the promotion of the licensing objectives):

(a) modify the conditions of the certificate;
(b) exclude a qualifying club activity from the scope of the certificate;
(c) suspend the certificate for a period not exceeding three months; or
(d) withdraw the certificate.

The Summary Review procedure can also be used in respect of a Club Premises Certificate (see Ch.2 on premises licences).

2.6.1 *Fees*

The club premises certificate is subject to the same provisions for payment of an annual fee as a premises licence.

2.7 Withdrawal of a certificate

A club which ceases to meet the criteria to be a qualifying club can have the certificate withdrawn by the licensing authority. If a certificate is withdrawn because the club membership has fallen below the required minimum of 25 members, the withdrawal will not have effect until three months after the authority gives notice and does not have effect if, by the end of the three-month period, the membership has risen to at least the required minimum number (s.90).

2.8 General provisions

If any determination is made by the local authority which amends a certificate, the council has a duty to amend the certificate and, if necessary, issue a new summary of it (s.93(1)).

The secretary of a club has a duty to ensure that the certificate—or a certified copy of it—is kept at the club premises. The person responsible for looking after the certificate is the secretary or a person nominated by the secretary (s.94).

A police constable, or an authorised officer of the licensing or fire authority, can enter a premises which has a club premises certificate, or in respect of which an application for a variation or a review of the certificate relates, to inspect the premises, having given the club 48 hours' notice (s.96).

Where a club premises certificate is in force, a police constable may enter and search the premises if he has reasonable cause to believe that an offence concerning drugs (supplying drugs, offering to supply drugs, being concerned with the supply of drugs or making an offer to supply drugs) has been, is being or is about to be committed there, or that there is likely to be a breach of the peace (s.97).

Chapter 3

Personal Licences

3.1 When is a personal licence required?

A personal licence is required to enable a person to supply or authorise the supply of alcohol in accordance with a premises licence (s.111).

3.2 How long will a licence last?

A personal licence will last for a period of ten years and can be renewed for further periods of ten years at a time. The licence will continue for the ten-year period unless it is surrendered or it is revoked or forfeited because the licensee has a conviction for a relevant offence (ss.115, 116, 124 and 129).

3.3 Application for a personal licence

The application must, if the person applying is ordinarily resident in the area of a licensing authority, be made to that authority. In any other case, if a person is not ordinarily resident in any area, an application can be made to any licensing authority (s.117).

A person can only hold one personal licence at any time and, while an application is being considered by a licensing authority, they cannot make another application until the initial application has been determined or withdrawn (s.118).

Individuals must meet the following criteria to apply for a personal licence:

(1) They must be aged 18 or over.

(2)   They must possess a licensing qualification accredited by
      the Secretary of State or be a person of a prescribed
      description.
      Currently the only person of a prescribed description is a
      person connected with the Commonality of the Vintners of
      London.
(3)   They must not have had a personal licence forfeited in the
      previous five years.
      If an applicant fails to meet criteria 1, 2 or 3, the local
      authority **must** reject the application.
(4)   They must not have been convicted of any relevant
      offences (or comparable foreign offences).

If an applicant has been convicted of a relevant offence, the
licensing authority must inform the police who can, within
fourteen days of being notified by the licensing authority, serve
a notice stating that they are satisfied that to grant a licence
would undermine the crime prevention objective (s.120).

If the police do serve a notice objecting to the applicant, the
licensing authority must hold a hearing unless the applicant,
the police and the licensing authority agree it is not necessary
to do so.

In connection with a police objection notice in the case of *R. (on
the application of South Northamptonshire Council) v Towcester
Magistrates Court* (February 6, 2008) the Judge said "The Chief
Constable bore no burden of demonstrating that the offence
would lead to an unacceptable risk of non-compliance. He had
to object to the grant if he was satisfied that the grant would
undermine the crime prevention objective. It is the applicant
who had to show why the grant to him would not undermine
it."

3.4 Application for renewal

At the end of a ten-year period, the applicant must apply to renew his licence. The application to renew must be made no earlier than three months nor later than one month before the licence is due to expire (s.117(6)).

For example, a personal licence granted on August 1, 2008 will expire on July 31, 2018. An application for renewal, therefore, must be made between May 1 and June 30, 2018.

If the application is not made within this period, the licence expires. As with an original application for a personal licence, only the police can object on the grounds that a crime prevention objective will be undermined. The police can only inform the licensing authority that they wish to object if the person has been convicted of a relevant offence (or comparable foreign offence) since the licence was granted or renewed (s.121).

3.5 How is an application made?

The Regulations prescribe the form of the application and precisely what has to be supplied (s.133).

The applicant must submit the following to the local authority:

(a) the application form;
(b) the fee;
(c) two photographs one endorsed as a true likeness—see reg.7(1) and the application form for details of the form of photograph;
(d) either:
    (i) a criminal conviction certificate issued under s.112 of the Police Act 1997;
    (ii) a criminal record certificate issued under s.113A of the Police Act 1997; or

    (iii) the results of a subject access search under the Data Protection Act 1998 of the Police National Computer by the National Identification Service.

The certificate or search results shall be issued no earlier than one month before the granting of the application.

In addition, the applicant must declare either that he has, or has not, been convicted of a relevant offence or foreign offence.

3.6   Form of licence

The licence issued by the licensing authority will be in a form specified by the Secretary of State and will be in two parts.

The first part will specify the holder's name and address and identify the licensing authority which granted it. In addition, it must contain a photograph of the holder, a number allocated by the licensing authority that is unique to the licence, an identifier for the licensing authority granting the licence and the date of expiry. This part must be in a durable form and no larger than 70mm x 100mm.

The second part of the licence must contain, if appropriate, a record of each relevant and foreign offence of which the licence holder has been convicted, including the date of conviction and the sentence imposed, together with the matters in the first part of the licence except the photograph.

3.7   Convictions during application period

If an applicant for a licence is convicted of a relevant (or comparable foreign) offence after the application has been made but before it has been determined, they must inform the licensing authority concerned. When this happens, the licensing authority must inform the police who must, if they are satisfied that to grant the licence would undermine the crime prevention objective, give the authority a notice to that effect within a period of fourteen days. The licensing authority will then hold a hearing to decide whether or not to grant the licence.

Should a conviction which occurred during the application period come to light after the licence has been granted or renewed then the police can consider whether revocation of the licence should be sought. If revocation is sought this must be considered by the licensing authority who must decide if revocation is necessary for the promotion of the crime prevention objective. This power is contained in s.24(4)(b) of the 2003 Act and is the only circumstances under that a licencing authority can revoke a personal licence.

This procedure of notifying the police and considering whether or not to refuse the application or revoke the licence would also apply where the convictions came to light some other way, e.g. a newspaper report.

3.8   Convictions after personal licence has been granted

Should a personal licence holder be charged with a relevant offence then, no later than the time they make their first appearance in court, they must produce their personal licence or, if that is not possible, tell the court that they hold a personal licence and which local authority issued it (s.128).

If a person is convicted of a relevant offence, the court can order the forfeiture of the personal licence or suspend it for a period of up to six months. The convicting court can suspend such an order to allow the licence to continue in force pending an appeal (s.128). Similarly, the court must notify the local authority that issued the personal licence of the conviction (s.131).

Should a court not be aware of the existence of a personal licence, the licensee is under a duty to inform the licensing authority as soon as possible of their conviction (s.128).

3.9   Relevant offences

Relevant offences under this Act are detailed in Appendix A and include licensing offences, and those related to theft, drink driving, sexual misconduct, violence and drugs misuse.

3.10   Foreign offences

In addition to informing the licensing authority of any relevant offences, an applicant for a personal licence, or a person holding a personal licence, must inform the authority if they have any foreign offences or if, during the currency of a licence, they are convicted of any such offences. A foreign offence means an offence, other than a relevant offence, under the law of any place outside England and Wales.

It is clear from the Act (for example, s.120(5)(b)) that a foreign offence will only be of concern to the police if it is comparable to a relevant offence.

3.11   Obligations of a personal licence holder

If a personal licence holder loses their licence or it is stolen, damaged or destroyed they must apply to the licensing authority for a copy of the licence (s.126).

Should a personal licence holder change their name or address, they must tell the licensing authority responsible for issuing the licence as soon as is reasonably practicable (s.127).

A personal licence holder is under a duty to produce their licence when requested to do so by a police constable or authorised officer from the licensing authority. Section 35(1) makes it clear that this power only applies to a personal licence holder who is on premises to make or authorise the supply of alcohol and such supplies are:

(a) authorised by a premises licence in respect of these premises; or

(b) a permitted temporary activity on the premises, of which he is the premises user, by virtue of a temporary event notice.

As can be seen, the police and authorised licensing authority officers have no right to require the production of a personal licence outside the premises concerned, nor can they ask to see the licence of a personal licence holder who is not making or authorising sales, e.g. who is off duty or engaged in other activities.

It should be noted that a personal licence holder requested to produce his personal licence by an authorised officer can request that officer to produce evidence of his authority to exercise this power (s.135(3)). If the officer fails to do this, the personal licence holder is under no legal obligation to produce his licence.

Chapter 4

Designated Premises Supervisor

One of the mandatory conditions of a premises licence which authorises the sale of alcohol is that there must be a designated premises supervisor. No supply of alcohol may be made on the premises unless there is a designated premises supervisor who holds a personal licence (s.19). Any sale of alcohol at a time when there is not a designated premises supervisor in place would be unlawful.

Procedures relating to the appointment and changes of designated premises supervisor are detailed in Ch.1, "Premises Licences".

The precise role of this person is not detailed in the Act. However, the guidance indicates that this person will be the person nominated by the premises licence holder as being the person responsible for day-to-day control of the licensed premises. (It is possible for the premises licence holder, if an individual, to also be the designated premises supervisor).

The statutory guidance also indicates that the designated premises supervisor will provide a single point of accountability in the event of problems occurring at the premises. As Lord Mackintosh stated, on behalf of the government and speaking in the House of Lords: "The designation tells the police who is in charge." However, there is no requirement for the premises supervisor to be present on the premises at all times.

It is, of course, possible for the Licensing Authority at a Review Hearing to attach an additional condition to the premises licence requiring the presence of the Designated Premises Supervisor at certain times if it was considered appropriate to promote the licensing objectives. Any such condition would of course, have to provide for absences caused by holiday and sickness.

There may be a number of personal licence holders on the premises but there will only be one designated premises supervisor, who will be easily identifiable as providing the sole point of accountability.

It is quite clear from the statutory guidance that the government intends the designated premises supervisor to be a position of some responsibility. This is why the person nominated has to consent to the appointment. Anyone so nominated would be advised to undertake appropriate training and obtain an appropriate qualification, such as the Award for Designated Premises Supervisors.

4.1 Community premises and the premises supervisor

Section 19 of the 2003 Act requires all premises licensed for the sale of alcohol to have a premises supervisor and for all sales of alcohol to be made or authorised by a person who holds a premises licence. The law was changed in 2009 to enable the management committee of a community premises to apply to have these particular mandatory conditions imposed under s.19 removed from their licence. If the application is successful then the management committee will be collectively responsible for ensuring compliance with the legislation and licence conditions.

There is a prescribed application form which requires the management committee to set out how the premises are managed, the committee structure and how the supervision of alcohol sales is to be ensured in different situations, and how responsibility for this is to be determined in individual cases and reviewed within the committee procedure in the event of nay issues arising. If the authority has any concerns they can ask the management committee for more information.

Community premises include church halls, chapels, also community halls and village halls. The main consideration in deciding if premises are community premises then consideration has to be given to how the premises are predominately used e.g.:

(i)   if they are genuinely made available for the community benefit most of the time; and
(ii) are accessible by a broad range of persons and sectors of the local community;
(iii) for purposes which include purposes beneficial to the community as a whole.

Chapter 5

Temporary Event Notices

5.1   Introduction

Unlike previous licensing regimes, there is no specific provision for occasional licences. It is possible to obtain a premises licence on a time-limit basis; this is the nearest thing to an occasional licence. However, the procedure for obtaining a time-limited premises licence is the same as for a permanent premises licence. Consequently, there is little commercial benefit in obtaining such a time-limited licence.

However, the Act does provide for what the government has called a "light touch" regime for events of limited duration held in small premises: temporary event notices. For these, permission is not needed but notice has to be given to the licensing authority, police and environmental health authority.

Temporary event notices can be used in respect of both completely unlicensed premises and licensed premises. For example, premises licensed only for the retail sale of alcohol could use a temporary event notice to authorise the staging of a darts championship without the need to vary the premises licence.

5.2   Limitations to temporary event notices

Temporary event notices are subject to various limitations. These are concerned with:

(1) **Duration**—they are limited to events lasting for up to 168 hours.
(2) **Scale**—they cannot involve the presence of more than 499 people at any one time.

59

The application form approved by Parliament as part of The Licensing Act 2003 (Permitted Temporary Activities) (Notices) Regulations 2005 indicates that the maximum figure of 499 "includes, for example, staff, organisers, stewards and performers".

(3) **Use of the same premises**—the same premises cannot be used more than 12 times, or more than a total of 21 days, in a single period of 12 months.

(4) **The number of notices given by one individual within a given period of time**—a personal licence holder is limited to 50 notices (including late TEN's) in a calendar year and a person who does not hold a personal licence to 5 notices (including late TEN's) in a similar period. In respect of a person who does not hold a personal licence, a notice given by an associate in the same year counts against them. An 'associate' includes:

(a) spouse;

(b) child, parent, grandchild, brother or sister of that person;

(c) agent or employee;

(d) the spouse of a person within (b) or (c).

The holder of a personal licence can serve 10 late TENs in a calendar year; a person who does not hold a personal licence is entitled to two late TENs in the same period. It should be noted that if the person serving the late TENs serves their total entitlement of late notices before they have used up their allocation of 50 or 10, no more Ordinary TENs can be served in that calendar year.

As indicated earlier, the most important aspects of the system of temporary event notices are that no permission is required for these events. In general, only the police and environmental health may intervene to prevent such an event taking place or to modify the arrangements for such an event and then only to prevent a licensing objective being undermined. A licensing authority can only intervene itself if the limits on the number of notices that may be given in various circumstances would be exceeded.

5.3   Service of notice

The temporary event notice that has to be served on the licensing authority together with the fee, with copies to the police and environmental health authority,, must be in the form prescribed by the Secretary of State and must contain the following information:

(a)   the licensable activities to take place during the event;
(b)   the period (not exceeding 168 hours) in which it is proposed to use the premises for licensable activities;
(c)   the times during the event period that the premises user proposes that the licensable activities shall take place;
(d)   the maximum number of persons (less than 500) which it is proposed should, during those times, be allowed on the premises at the same time;
(e)   where the licensable activities include the supply of alcohol, whether the supplies are proposed to be for consumption on the premises or off the premises or both; and
(f)   any other matters prescribed by the Secretary of State.

On each occasion, at least ten working days' notice must be given, but there is nothing to prevent simultaneous notification of multiple events at a single time so long as the final event is at least ten days away.

Where the licensable activities include the supply of alcohol, the notice must make it a condition of using the premises that all supplies are made by, or under the authority of, the person giving the temporary event notice.

It is one of the oddities of the Act that five times a year a person who is not a personal licence holder and who may have no knowledge of licensing law can retail alcohol.

The police and the environmental health authority can serve an objection notice if it is considered that a licensing objective would be undermined. Any objection notice must be served within three working days of the notification. If the police do not intervene, they will still be able to exercise their powers of closure should disturbance or disorder subsequently arise (see Ch.6). Similarly, if the environmental health authority does not serve an objection notice they can still exercise their powers under other legislation should problems subsequently arise.

An objection notice that has not been withdrawn has to be considered at a licensing hearing unless all parties consider it unnecessary.

At the licensing hearing, the licensing authority can issue a counter notice (which effectively cancels the temporary event notice), if it is appropriate for the promotion of a licensing objective.

The licensing authority can also issue a counter notice if the various limits (e.g. 168 hours) are exceeded (ss.100–107).

Where a temporary event notice has been given, a police constable or an authorised officer may, at any reasonable time, enter the premises which are the subject of the notice (s.108).

The person serving the notice on the licensing authority must ensure that it together with any statement of conditions is prominently displayed at the premises. Alternatively, the notice together with any statement of conditions may be kept in the custody of the premises user or in the custody of a person nominated by him. Such a person must be present and working at the premises. Where the notice is held by a nominated person, a notice specifying this fact and the position held by the nominated person must be prominently displayed at the premises (s.109).

Where a temporary event notice acknowledged by the licensing authority is lost, stolen, damaged or destroyed, the premises user can ask the licensing authority for a copy of the notice. The authority must issue a copy of the notice if they are satisfied that it has been lost, stolen, damaged or destroyed and, where it was lost or stolen, the matter has been reported to the police (s.110).

The requirement to serve the TEN in duplicate is removed by the 2011 Act. Instead the licensing authority will have to acknowledge in writing receipt of the notice.

5.4 Late TENs

The 2011 Act introduced Late Temporary Event Notices with effect from April 25, 2012. Late TENs are notices served:

(a) electronically to the licensing authority, no earlier than nine working days before the event and no later than five working days before the event begins;

(b) in writing to the licensing authority, police and the environmental health authority no later than five working days before the event begins and to at least one of those no earlier than nine working days before the event begins.

The holder of a premises licence can serve ten Late TENs in a calendar year and a non-personal licence holder two Late TENS in the same period.

5.4.1 *Service of counter notices*

The Licensing Act 2003 (Permitted Temporary Activities) (Notices) Regulations 2005 state that a counter notice is given in the prescribed manner if it is:

(a) delivered to the relevant premises user in person;

(b) left at the appropriate address;

(c) sent to that address by ordinary post; or

(d) sent by e-mail to an appropriate e-mail address.

5.4.2 *Conditions*

Normally conditions cannot be attached to a Temporary Events Notice. This means that, in certain circumstances, a TEN served in respect of licensed premises could mean that conditions on the premises licence would have no effect whilst the premises are operating under the authority of the TEN.

The 2011 Act, however, changed this slightly. Where an objection has been lodged to a standard TEN and the Licensing Authority decides not to issue a counter notice the Authority can, if appropriate to the promotion of the Licensing Objectives, impose one or more conditions on the TEN. Such conditions can only be those already imposed on a premises licence or club premises certificate and they must not be inconsistent with the carrying out of the activities authorised by the TEN.

5.5 Appeals

There is **no right of appeal** where a counter notice is issued because various limits have been exceeded, for example where a personal licence holder has already given 50 temporary event notices in that calendar year or where premises have already been used for 15 days in that year. However, if as a result of a police or environmental health authority objection the relevant licensing authority issues a counter notice prohibiting an event, the premises user has the right to appeal.

If the police object to a temporary event notice, but the licensing authority does not issue a counter notice, the police have the right to appeal against this decision.

In both cases, the appeal must be made to the Magistrates' Court within 21 days commencing on the day on which the licensing authority notified the appellant of its decision to issue/not to issue a counter notice, as appropriate.

No appeal may be brought later than five working days before the first day of the event period specified.

If the police or environmental health authority object to a late Temporary Event Notice the event cannot go ahead. There is no right to a hearing before the licensing authority and no appeal to the magistrates court.

Chapter 6

Sale and supply of alcohol to children

6.1 Introduction

The previous legislation gave the impression that alcohol and children did not go together. It is true that is was possible to obtain a children's certificate but such conditions were often riddled with conditions that made usage uneconomic.

In contrast, the Licensing Act 2003 contains no general prohibition on the admission of children to licensed premises (with one exception that will be mentioned later). It is up to the premises licence holder to decide whether or not children should be allowed on licensed premises and under what conditions. However, the licence holder will of course have to include appropriate measures in his operating schedule to promote the licensing objective of protecting children from harm.

Furthermore, the Act contains a number of restrictions and prohibitions on the sale to, and the consumption of, alcohol by persons under 18.

6.2 Unaccompanied children prohibited from certain premises

Section 145 of the Act makes it an offence to allow children under the age of 16, who are not accompanied by an adult, to be present:

- On premises used exclusively or primarily for the supply of alcohol for consumption on those premises, when they are open for such supplies.
- At other premises licensed for alcohol consumption on the premises, between **midnight and 5am** when open for alcohol supplies. (An example of such a premises would be a restaurant where consumption of alcohol is secondary to dining—at these premises unaccompanied children could be present outside these hours.)

It should be noted that this provision applies not only to licensed premises but also to those operating under a club premises certificate or a temporary event notice.

It should also be noted that no offence is committed if the unaccompanied child is on the premises solely for the purpose of going to or coming from another place, to or from which there is no other convenient route (s.145(5)). An example would be a child having to pass through the premises to get to the toilet.

6.3 Sale of alcohol to children

Section 146 makes it a criminal offence for any person to sell alcohol anywhere to a person who is under the age of 18. **There are no exceptions.**

By s.147 it is an offence to knowingly allow the sale of alcohol to someone aged under 18. This offence can be committed by anyone who works at the premises (including club premises) in a capacity that would have allowed them to prevent the sale.

6.4 Sale of liqueur confectionery to children

It is an offence to sell liqueur confectionery to a person aged under 16 (s.148).

6.5   Consumption of alcohol by children

Persons under the age of 18 generally cannot consume alcohol on licensed premises (including premises with a club premises certificate). It is also an offence for a member of staff at the premises to knowingly allow children to consume alcohol (s.150). There is one exception: a 16 or 17 year-old is allowed to drink beer, wine or cider with a table meal *provided* that an adult purchases the drink and that an adult accompanies the 16 or 17-year old at the table meal.

6.6   Purchase of alcohol by or on behalf of children

Section 149 makes it an offence for anyone under the age of 18 to purchase or attempt to purchase alcohol, or for someone over the age of 18 to purchase or attempt to purchase alcohol on behalf of someone under 18 (apart from the table meal exception mentioned above).

6.7   Delivering alcohol to children

Section 151 makes it an offence for someone working on licensed premises (including club premises) to knowingly deliver to someone aged under 18 alcohol sold or supplied on the premises.

It is also an offence for a person working on such premises, who is in a position which gives him authority to prevent the delivery, to knowingly allow that delivery to take place. Thus, if a person authorises the delivery of alcohol to a young person, knowing him or her to be under the age of 18, an offence takes place.

However, s.151(6) provides that no offence is committed if a young person merely signs for alcohol delivered to a home or place of work, provided that an adult placed the order. Equally, an individual who is under 18 years old may collect a delivery on behalf of his employer.

6.8   Sending a child to obtain alcohol

Section 152 makes it is an offence to knowingly send a young person to obtain alcohol that is sold for consumption off the premises or alcohol supplied in a club for such consumption. The offence applies whether the young person is sent to the actual premises where the alcohol is sold or supplied, or to other premises to which the alcohol has been sent.

6.9   Prohibition of unsupervised sales by children

Section 153 makes it an offence to knowingly allow a person aged under 18 to sell or supply alcohol on licensed premises (e.g. a young person serving behind a bar or working on the till in a supermarket), unless:

(a)   each such sale or supply is specifically approved by a premises licence holder or designated premises supervisor (but not, strangely, any other personal licence holder); or

(b)   each and every such sale is approved by another person aged over 18 who is so authorised by the licence holder or designated premises supervisor.

It is not, however, an offence for such a young person to sell or deliver alcohol for consumption with a table meal. In effect, a person under 18 working as a waiter or waitress is able to serve alcohol.

6.10   Enforcement of age related sales provisions

Section 154 makes it a positive duty of weights and measures authorities to enforce the provisions relating to the sale of alcohol to children. Furthermore, they can seek to detect such offences by the use of 'test purchasing'.

This means that the police and weights and measures inspectors (trading standards officers) are empowered to send individuals who are under the age of 18 years into licensed premises to attempt to buy alcohol. Neither the actions of such officers nor the young people involved constitute offences under the Act (s.152(4)).

6.11   Defences

If a person is charged with selling alcohol to someone aged under the age of 18 years, it is a defence to show that:

(a)   he believed that the individual was aged 18 or over; and
(b)   either:
   (i)   he had taken all reasonable steps to establish the individual's age, or
   (ii)   nobody could reasonably have suspected from the individual's appearance that they were aged under 18.

A person is to be considered to have taken all reasonable steps to establish an individual's age if:

(a)   he asked the individual for evidence of his age; and
(b)   the evidence would have convinced a reasonable person.

The same defence is available to persons charged with an offence of allowing a child under the age of 16 to be on licensed premises when not accompanied by an adult or in relation to the sale of liqueur confectionery to children under 16.

When a person is charged with offences under these provisions by reason of the act or default of some other person, it is a defence that the person charged has exercised all due diligence to avoid the offence being committed. That is one reason why personal licence holders authorising other persons to sell alcohol on their behalf are advised to ensure that the persons concerned are appropriately trained.

The High Court considered the due diligence defence in *Croydon LBC v Pinch a Pound (UK) Ltd* (2011) L.L.R. 19. The case involved selling a knife to a 15 year old boy. The company ran the "due diligence" defence. The High Court held the defence requires proof of two elements—the taking of all reasonable precautions and the exercise of due diligence. The company must take all reasonable precautions to avoid the commission of the offence by their employees i.e. have a system in place and train the staff. However, the company must go further and exercise all due diligence by ensuring the measures put in place are maintained, adhered to by the employees and continue to be adequate in the context of the risk of which the statute is aimed at and the nature of the business.

6.12   Persistently selling alcohol to children

A responsible person, (defined as the premises licence holder or the premises user under a TEN), is guilty of an offence if on two or more different occasions within a period of three consecutive months alcohol is sold on the same premises to a person under 18. The penalty on conviction is a maximum fine of £20,000. If the person convicted is the premises licence holder the Court can order that the part of the premises licence which authorises alcohol sales be suspended for up to three months.

It should be noted that person making the unauthorised sales does not have to be the same person on each occasion. Furthermore in determining whether the two or more unauthorised sales have taken place not only convictions are taken into account but also police cautions and fixed penalty fines.

In certain circumstances the police (superintendent or above) or a weights and measures inspector can instead of prosecuting offer "voluntary" closure for a period of between 48 and 336 hours of their choosing. If such closure is accepted this wipes the slate clean for those offences (ss.169A and B).

6.13   Preventing underage purchases

As indicated in Ch.1 (premises licences) a mandatory condition attached to the premises licence requires premises to have an age verification policy in place, requiring all staff to check the identity of anyone appearing to be under the age of 18 years (or such older age as may be indicated in the policy). It is, therefore, vital that if there is any doubt about a person's age that ID is asked for and checked thoroughly. Many licensees have found the challenge 21 or challenge 25 initiatives helpful. These require staff to ask customers to prove they are over 18 if they appear to be under 21 or 25. Exhibiting a "No proof, no sale" notice may also be helpful.

Generally speaking, staff will have been regarded as "exercising all due diligence" by asking for proof of age from any person about whose age there is doubt.

Documentary evidence can be:

- A photo driving licence.
- A passport.
- A proof of age scheme card which carries the PASS logo.

Schemes accredited by the PASS scheme have the advantage that PASS scheme proof of age cards carry a hologram, which makes them more difficult to forge.

Chapter 7

Hearings

7.1 Introduction

There are a number of references to hearings in the Licensing Act 2003. Essentially, whenever relevant representations or objections are made to an application, or if an application has been made for a review of a premises licence, a hearing has to be held, unless all parties consider it unnecessary.

This chapter concentrates on what happens when relevant representations are made to an application for a premises licence. In this chapter the term "Regulations" refers to the Licensing Act 2003 (Hearings) Regulations 2005 (SI 2005/44), as amended by the Licensing Act 2003 (Hearings) (Amendment) Regulations 2005 (SI 2005/78).

7.2 What happens before a hearing?

Normally, a hearing has to be commenced within 20 working days of the end of the period for making representations. However, reg.11 gives the licensing authority power to extend this time limit for a specified period where it considers it necessary in the public interest. If this power is exercised, the authority must give a notice to this effect to all the parties concerned, stating the reason for the extension.

7.3 Conciliation

Some enlightened licensing authorities will seek to mediate between an applicant for a premises licence and those making relevant representations with a view to avoid a hearing. This can be done by correspondence, or by convening a meeting between the parties with an officer of the licensing authority acting as an impartial chairman. This officer will not be there to make decisions but to try and facilitate an agreement between the parties.

It may be that that the applicant, having considered the representations, may want to offer additional safeguards or conditions to address the concerns of those making representations. In some cases, the applicant may wish to consider amending the application. Equally, it may be that those making representations, having considered the additional safeguards, etc. being offered, will be prepared to withdraw their representations or to agree that a hearing is no longer necessary.

The experience of those authorities that have conciliation procedures is that mediation meetings are very useful. In a large number of cases agreement can be reached. Even where full agreement cannot be achieved, often the areas of disagreement are significantly reduced, leading to shorter and more focused hearings.

7.4   Preparation for hearings

If conciliation fails or is not attempted, a hearing has to be arranged.

The licensing authority will arrange a date, time and place for the hearing. If the authority considers that the hearing might extend into a second day, they have to ensure that the two days of the hearing are held on consecutive working days.

At the same time, an officer of the licensing authority should be studying the application with its operating schedule and the letters of representation to see if there will be points on which clarification will be needed from a party at the hearing.

This having been done, the licensing authority has to give notice of the hearing to the parties concerned. This notice has to be given no later than 10 working days before the day, or first day, of the hearing.

The notice has to contain the following information:

- The rights of the parties at a hearing.
- The consequences if a party does not attend or is not represented at the hearing.
- The procedure to be followed at the hearing.
- Any particular points on which the authority considers it will want clarification at a hearing.

The notice to the applicant must be accompanied by the letters of representation (unless of course they were supplied earlier as part of the conciliation process).

7.5   Action by the parties on receipt of the notice

No later than five working days before the day, or first day, of the hearing, each party shall give a notice to the licensing authority stating:

(1) Whether he intends to attend or be represented at the hearing.
(2) Whether he considers a hearing to be unnecessary.

If a party wishes another person (other than a person he intends to represent him) to appear at a hearing, the notice must contain a request for permission for that person to appear at the hearing. The request should give the name of the person and explain briefly the point, or points, on which the person may be able to assist the authority in respect of the application or representation.

For example, an applicant might want a specialist to explain the practical steps being taken to prevent disturbance to residents. A residents' association might want to call a resident to give first-hand evidence of his/her experiences.

The request has to be renewed at the commencement of the hearing. Regulation 22 indicates that such a request should not be unreasonably refused.

7.6 Right to dispense with a hearing if all parties agree

If all parties agree that a hearing is unnecessary, the licensing authority can dispense with a hearing. This is most likely to happen where conciliation action has been taken by the authority. The parties have to confirm in writing that they consider a hearing to be unnecessary and the authority in turn has to give written notice to the parties that the hearing has been dispensed with.

7.7 Withdrawal of the representations

Any party who wishes to withdraw their representations may do so. This may be done in advance by giving a notice to the authority no later than 24 hours before the day, or first day, of the hearing. In some cases this could lead to the cancellation of the hearing.

Alternatively, the representation could be withdrawn orally at the hearing—this might be as a result of additional safeguards or conditions offered by the applicant either immediately prior to, or at, the hearing.

7.8 Adjournment of a hearing

The Regulations give the licensing authority power to adjourn a hearing to a specified date where it is necessary for its consideration of the representations of any party.

For example, it might seem immediately prior to a hearing that the parties could come to an agreement which would make a hearing unnecessary. Even if agreement was not in fact reached, the basis of the representations might be changed. The hearing could, in these circumstances, be adjourned to allow time for this possibility to be pursued. Another example might be where a party is ill and the authority deems it necessary, in order to consider the application or representation properly, for that person to be present.

The licensing authority also has power to arrange for a hearing to be held on specified additional dates. This might be where the authority considers the matter to be unusually complex, or where earlier cases had taken longer than expected, i.e. in cases where it would be impossible to complete the hearing on the original date. In these circumstances, rather than start a hearing that could not be completed, the hearing would be adjourned to another day or days. (If the hearing would run for more than one day, the days selected must, of course, be consecutive working days (reg.5).)

In *Hammersmith & Fulham LBC v Food City Express Ltd* (2010) L.L.R. 292 the High Court considered the situation where an applicant did not attend and the Sub-Committee proceeded with the hearing. The applicant arrived just as the decision was announced to vary the hours of the premises licence but not granting the 24 hours opening for the sale of alcohol applied for. The District Judge allowed the Company's appeal holding that there had not been a fair hearing as the members had only waited 10 minutes before beginning the hearing. The High Court allowed the authority's appeal holding that the licensing committee had followed reg.20 of the Hearings Regulations as, before proceeding with the hearing, they did consider whether it was necessary in the public interest to adjourn and considered it was not. The High Court also held that the District Judge was wrong in holding there had been an unfair hearing because the Sub-Committee only waited 10 minutes for the applicant to arrive. The Judge held this was an irrelevant factor to take into account. The period they decided to wait for the applicant was a matter for the sub-committee members.

7.9   Committee report

Shortly before a hearing, a council officer should prepare a report to the sub-committee determining the application. This enables the sub-committee to acquaint themselves with the basic facts of the case, saving time at the hearing.

A basic format of a committee report might appear as follows.

7.9.1   *The application*

This is a summary of the nature of the application, licensable activities, hours, supply of alcohol, etc.

7.9.2   *Background*

Any relevant background information might be included.

7.9.3   *The promotion of licensing objectives*

Details of the promotion of the four licensing objectives might be included:

(1)   The prevention of crime and disorder.
(2)   Public safety.
(3)   The prevention of public nuisance.
(4)   The protection of children from harm.

7.9.4   *Relevant representations*

Details of relevant representations received in relation to the four licensing objectives might be included.

7.9.5 Interested parties

Details of representations made by interested parties might be included.

7.9.6 Policy considerations

Details of relevant policy considerations might be given, including a local policy statement, particularly any relevant part of the authorities statement of licensing policy and relevant statutory guidance from the Secretary of State.

7.9.7 Associated papers

Details of appendices might be given. These should normally include copies of representations received.

7.10 Rights of a party at a hearing

In general, a party may attend a hearing and may be assisted or represented by any person, whether or not that person is legally qualified. Generally, an applicant might want to be represented by a solicitor or barrister, but a resident might want to be represented by a ward councillor or an officer of his residents' association.

7.11 What happens at a hearing?

The procedure at a hearing is at the discretion of the licensing authority concerned. However, as any hearing has to conform to the Regulations, the discretion of the authority is rather limited.

At the beginning of the hearing, the authority has to explain to the parties the procedure to be followed at the hearing and, as explained earlier, it will consider any request for another person to appear at the hearing.

Regulation 23 states that the hearing shall take the form of a discussion led by the authority. Cross-examination will not normally be permitted, unless the authority considers it necessary for the consideration of the application or representations. This does not sit easily with reg.24, which states that the authority must allow the parties an equal maximum period of time in which to exercise their rights.

A discussion-led hearing is a totally different style of hearing, and was not the subject of any consultation whatsoever by the government. It is expected that there will be a number of different ways that authorities will try to conduct this style of hearing.

The equal maximum period of time could cause difficulty and unfairness if not dealt with sensibly by the licensing authority. Let us suppose, for example, that an application for a premises licence has attracted 30 relevant representations. All the persons making representations have attended the hearing and wish to speak. They, together with the applicant, are parties to the hearing. If the applicant is allowed 10 minutes, each person making relevant representations is allowed 10 minutes— totalling, in this case, 300 minutes, or five hours! This hardly seems fair on the applicant.

One suggested form of procedure that could be used is set out below:

- The Chair opens the meeting, introducing members of the committee and officers present to the applicant and members of the public. The Chair explains the nature of the decision to be taken and the procedure to be followed.
- The officer outlines the application, any relevant representations and any relevant part of the authority licensing policy statement and/or statutory guidance from the Secretary of State.
- Members ask any relevant questions of the officer.
- Any party that has requested permission for another person to appear at the hearing renews their request.
- The sub-committee decides on the request.

- The licensing officer (or other appropriate officer) intro-duces the applicant (if present) and invites him or her, or the person representing them, to address the committee or to clarify any information previously requested.
- The licensing officer (or other appropriate officer) invites those parties making representations to address the sub-committee.

Note. Where there are a number of parties addressing the same or similar issues, it may be helpful for them to nominate a spokesman to speak on their behalf to avoid unnecessary repetition.

- Members ask any relevant questions of those parties making representations.
- If granted permission by the sub-committee, the applicant or the person representing them asks questions of those parties making representations.
- If necessary, the sub-committee will consider requests to allow other persons invited by the applicant to address the committee.
- The applicant or the person representing them addresses the sub-committee.
- Members may ask any relevant questions of the applicant or the person representing them.
- If granted permission by the sub-committee, parties that made representations ask any relevant questions of the applicant or the person representing them.
- The Chair invites the applicant or those representing them, and any parties making representations, to briefly summa-rise their points if they wish.
- Chair asks all parties whether they are satisfied that they have said all they wish to.
- Members of the committee discuss and make their decision (usually in closed session).
- The Chair relays the decision and the reasons given for the decision, as well as any conditions placed upon the licence (if granted) and the licensing objective(s) that they relate to.

7.12   Disruptive persons

The Regulations give the authority power to require any person attending the hearing, who in their opinion is behaving in a disruptive manner, to leave the hearing. In addition, they may:

(a)   refuse to permit that person to return; or
(b)   permit him to return only on such conditions as the authority may specify.

A person who has been excluded from the hearing does have the right, before the hearing concludes, to submit in writing any information he would have been entitled to give orally if he had not been required to leave.

7.13   Natural justice and human rights

Any hearing must conform not only with the Regulations but also to the principles of natural justice and the relevant provisions of the Human Rights Act and the European Convention on Human Rights.

One simple, although not very precise, definition is that "natural justice is the normal human rights of a reasonable man". In other words, it is the justice that a normal person could reasonably expect.

7.13.1   *The evolution of natural justice*

In the case of *R. v Civil Service Appeal Board Ex p. Cunningham* (1991), the point was made that the rules of natural justice are not engraved on tablets of stone. The Court went on to make an important statement:

"... when statutory bodies make decisions affecting individuals, the courts will expect not only the statutory procedures to be followed **but will imply the introduction of additional safeguards to ensure the attainment of fairness**".

In other words, a licensing authority could follow the procedures laid down in the Regulations to the letter but, if the proceedings were unfair to a party, the authority could still find themselves the subject of a judicial review. This is because the courts will expect licensing authorities to ensure that their procedures are designed to ensure the attainment of fairness.

In *R. (on the application of Hope & Glory Public House Ltd) v City of Westminster Magistrates Court* (2011) L.L.R. 105 the Court of Appeal made the following comments on the approach of licensing Committees to licensing applications:

"The function of a licensing authority is an administrative function. By contrast the function of the appellate court is a judicial function. The licensing authority has a duty to behave fairly in the decision making procedure but the decision itself is not a judicial or quasi-judicial act. It is the exercise of a power delegated by the people as a whole to decide what the public interest requires. Licensing decisions often involve weighing a variety of competing considerations: the demand for licensed establishments, the economic benefit to proprietor and the locality in drawing in visitors and stimulating the demand; the effect on law and disorder; the impact on those who live and work in the vicinity and so on. Sometimes a decision may involve a narrower question, such as whether noise, noxious smells or litter coming from premises amount to a public nuisance. Although such questions are in a sense questions of fact they are not questions of the "heads or tails variety". They involve an evaluation of what is to be regarded as reasonably acceptable in the particular location. In any case deciding what (if any) conditions should be attached to a licence as necessary and proportionate to the promotion of the statutory licensing objectives is essentially a matter of judgment rather than a matter of fact."

7.14   Some key issues

7.14.1   *Applicant's right to be heard*

If refusal of an application is contemplated, the applicant must be given the right to be heard. The applicant has 'the right to know what is alleged against him and the right to be heard in his own cause', *Greater London Council v Langlian Ltd* (1977) Crown Court (Unreported).

An applicant has only to be given an opportunity to be heard. If an applicant does not wish to take advantage of that opportunity, he cannot complain about the manner in which a subsequent decision was taken.

Note . This applies even when criminal proceedings are pending. This principle was first established in *R. v The Gaming Licensing Committee for the North Westminster Licensing Division of Central London Ex p. The Victoria Sporting Club Ltd* (1980).

7.14.2   *Bias by the determining body must be avoided*

Note. In this connection, a person who has an interest in considering the matter must be disqualified from hearing it or even retiring with the determining body when they reach a decision (*R v Chesterfield BC Ex p. Darker Enterprises Ltd* (1992)).

Equally, **officers who are not impartial** must not be present when the adjudicating body makes its decision (*R v Barnsley Metropolitan BC Ex p. Hook* (1976)). This is why a licensing authority would be wise to resolve that normally only the legal adviser and the committee officer would accompany members of the sub-committee when they retire to reach their decision.

It should be noted that **not only bias but the appearance of bias** should be avoided.

In the case of *Hannam v Bradford City Council* (1970), the High Court ruled that it does not matter what actually happens in the committee room but what the impartial bystander looking in *thinks* may have happened. The point was reinforced in the case of *Costas Georgiou v Enfield LBC* April 7, 2004: " . . . a fair-minded and informed observer would conclude there was a real possibility of bias in the sense of decisions being taken with closed minds and without impartial consideration . . ."

7.14.3 Members' interest

Closely linked to the issue of bias are the interests of council members.

Councillors are bound by the Members' Code of Conduct. Failure to comply with the Code may result in:

(a) a complaint being made against the member to the Standards Board (England) or Ombudsman (Wales); or
(b) potential judicial review of the decision.

The Code states (in England):

- If a member has a personal interest, he/she must disclose that interest at the meeting or when it becomes apparent.
- If the personal interest is a prejudicial interest (that is, one which a member of the public with knowledge of the relevant facts would reasonably regard as so significant that it is likely to prejudice the member's judgment of the public interest), the member must:
  (i)   withdraw from the room (they must not remain even in a personal capacity); and
  (ii) refrain from seeking to improperly influence a decision about that matter.

This does not preclude the licensing committee or sub-committee from considering written relevant representations from a councillor where the councillor is personally affected by a licensing application. However, although the sub-committee can consider such representations, the councillor making the representations cannot be present in the committee room, as they would have a personal and prejudicial interest.

However, the Code does not appear to prevent a ward councillor from representing his or her constituents at a hearing—because of reg.15. This is provided, of course, that the member concerned does not have a personal and prejudicial interest in the matter.

7.14.4   Hearsay evidence

Hearsay evidence can be admitted at a licensing hearing and it is up to council members to determine how much weight to put on such evidence (*Westminster City Council v Zestfair Ltd* (1990)). Due to the fact that the Regulations state that cross-examination will not normally be permitted and witnesses will not necessarily be called, hearsay evidence may well become more frequent with this new type of hearing. Council members will need to learn how much weight to put on such evidence. In *McCool v Rushcliffe BC* (1998) 3 All E.R. 889 the High Court stated "hearsay might by its source, nature and inherent probability carry a greater degree of credibility than evidence given first hand. What is not allowed is gossip, speculation and unsubstantiated innuendo. All would depend on the particular facts and circumstances" These comments were confirmed in *Leeds City Council v Hussain* (2002) EWHC 1145.

7.15   The Human Rights Act 1998 and the European Convention on Human Rights (ECHR)

7.15.1   Introduction

The Human Rights Act (HRA) in effect incorporates into UK law the rights and freedoms set out in the European Convention on Human Rights. The main principles of the Act can be summarised as follows:

- It is unlawful for public authorities, including all courts and tribunals, to act in a way that is incompatible with the Convention.

- All legislation (primary, subordinate and whenever enacted) must be interpreted so as to be compatible with the Convention "so far as it is possible to do so".
- Where, even when applying the new rule of construction, it is simply not possible to interpret legislation so as to be compatible with the Convention, the higher courts can strike down subordinate legislation.

It should be noted that these courts have no power to strike down primary legislation, but may make a "declaration of incompatibility", which is intended to prompt government action.

7.15.2 *The principle of proportionality*

Inherent in the Convention is the need to find a fair balance between the protection of individual rights and the interests of the community at large. The principle of proportionality is concerned with defining that "fair balance".

According to the consistent case law of the European Court and Commission, a fair balance between the protection of individual rights and the interests of the community at large can be achieved only if restrictions on individual rights are strictly proportionate to the legitimate aim they pursue.

In other words, even where it is clear that there is a legitimate purpose for restricting a Convention right, the authorities must still show that the actual restriction employed does not go beyond what is strictly necessary to achieve that purpose.

In licensing terms, this means that an application should not necessarily be rejected even if there is sufficient evidence to do so. Instead, the sub-committee concerned should consider whether the licensing objectives could be achieved by additional safeguards or conditions, rather than by rejecting the application.

7.15.3   Fair hearing (art.6)

Article 6(1) provides:

> "In the determination of his civil rights and obligations or of any criminal charge against him, everyone is entitled to a fair and public hearing within a reasonable time by an independent and impartial tribunal established by law. Judgment shall be pronounced publicly."

The right to a "fair hearing" has been widely interpreted by the ECHR and will include a person having real and effective access to a court, an opportunity to present his case and being given a reasoned decision.

The overriding obligation is to ensure that proceedings are fair and that submissions, arguments and evidence have been properly examined. The government clearly believes that the Regulations achieve this but many people have considerable doubts.

The requirement that the tribunal is "impartial" is clearly linked with the independence of the tribunal but extends beyond this to include an absence of prejudice or bias.

"Hearing within a reasonable time": guidelines from European courts indicate that the factors to be taken into account are:

- The complexity of the case.
- What is at stake for the applicant.
- The conduct of the domestic authorities.
- The conduct of the applicant.

The Regulations lay down strict time limits but, in certain cases, the council will have power to extend those time limits. In extending time limits, the council should have regard to the factors mentioned.

7.15.4   *Equality of arms*

The European Court and Commission have long recognised that "equality of arms is an inherent element of a fair trial". In civil proceedings, "equality of arms" implies:

> ". . . that each party must be afforded a reasonable opportunity to present his case—including his evidence—under conditions that do not place him at a substantial disadvantage vis-à-vis his opponent." (*Dombo Beheer BV v Netherlands* (1994).)

As indicated earlier, this is one of the reasons why reg.24 could lead to unfairness if it meant that the applicant had considerably less time to present his case compared with the other parties at the hearing.

7.16   Conclusion

The government clearly intends there to be equality of arms in relation to licensing hearings, although the licensing sub-committee concerned will have to take care to ensure that it happens in practice. Unfortunately, as we have seen, this has been made more difficult by some of the Regulations.

The sub-committee will clearly be weighing the public interest, including the licensing objectives, against the rights of individuals (applicants and interested parties). Provided that the rules of natural justice and the requirements of ECHR are followed, the risk of a licensing authority facing a judicial review should be slight.

It must be borne in mind, however, that the licensing authority will always be party to an appeal. If a decision was made without evidence to support it, there is a strong risk that that the decision will be overturned—with the possibility of costs being awarded against the council. Whilst the Regulations indicate that cross-examination will not normally occur at a licensing hearing, at an appeal hearing before the Magistrates the evidence will almost certainly will be tested in this way.

Therefore, the licensing sub-committee may, when considering an application and representations and the need to promote the licensing objectives, feel it sensible to ensure that the evidence it has considered has been properly tested and will withstand scrutiny in the Magistrates' Court.

R. (on the application of Daniel Thwaites plc) v Wirral Borough Magistrates Court (2008) L.L.R. 536 involved local residents who made representations to an application for longer hours claiming that people would come from other licensed premises that closed earlier and they would cause problems. The authority granted the application with conditions. Following an appeal by the residents the Magistrates allowed overturned the decision holding that while there had not been any complaints about noise since the longer hours were granted, there was a possibility of migration from other public houses may take place leading to public nuisance and crime and disorder. The High Court overturned the Magistrates holding

(1) All regulatory action should only be taken where it is necessary to promote the licensing objectives
(2) Magistrates (and Councillors) are entitled to take into account their own knowledge but they must measure their own views against the evidence presented to them. They cannot presume that if people came from other premises they would be a problem
(3) The Magistrates proceeded without proper evidence and gave their own views excessive weight and their decision limited the hours of operation without it being established that it was necessary to do so to promote the licensing objectives.

7.17   Other licensing hearings

This chapter has concentrated on licensing hearings where an application for a premises licence has been the subject of relevant representations. There are a number of other situations where a hearing will be necessary, e.g. to consider an application to review a premises licence, or a police objection to a temporary event notice. The basic procedure will be the same but the time limits, the persons to be notified and the information to be supplied to the parties will be different.

Appendix B sets out the period of notice that has to be given for the various types of hearing; Appendix C the period of time within which a hearing must be commenced; Appendix D the persons to be given notice of a hearing; and Appendix E the documents that have to accompany notice of a hearing. Appendix F sets out the meaning given in the Regulations to the word "determination". Throughout these appendices, references to a section or a Schedule mean a reference to a section of, or Schedule to, the Act.

Chapter 8

Conditions

8.1 Introduction

At licensing hearings, a licensing authority has wide discretion as to what conditions can be attached to premises licences and club premises certificates. However, conditions can only be imposed on a licence or certificate if they are **appropriate for the promotion of the licensing objectives**. The 2011 Act replaced the word "necessary" with "appropriate". The word "necessary" means "really needed." It is clear that whether or not it is appropriate to, e.g. attach a condition is a lower evidential threshold. The word "appropriate is defined as " right or suitable, fitting." This may lead to a lot of discussion. If the members decide it is "appropriate" to attach a condition should their decision be accepted and not overturned on appeal?

Clearly there must be evidence before the members to justify a condition being attached to an authorisation. It would not be lawful for a condition to be attached to a licence simply because members considered it appropriate to do so when there was no evidence to justify the condition. An example of where a problem may arise is in the case of where the police ask for CCTV cameras in every licensed premises. Just because the police ask for this condition would it be an "appropriate" condition. Perhaps the courts will be asking where is the evidence to justify why CCTV cameras should be installed in these particular premises.

The promotion of the licensing objectives is the only reason that a condition can be imposed on a licence. If a condition is imposed on a licence that does not relate to one or more of the objectives, it would be *ultra vires* (outside the law). It could not be enforced in the courts and would be struck out on appeal.

Furthermore, the condition must be **appropriate** to promote the licensing objectives. If the condition is not essential to the promotion of the objectives, it should not be imposed. The question that a licensing authority should ask itself before imposing a condition is: "Would a licensing objective be undermined if this condition was not on the licence?"

A similar test should be applied by council officers when they are drafting licences where the application is not the subject of relevant representations. Here, however, the authority can also only attach conditions that are consistent with the operating schedule, if necessary (appropriate) to promote the licensing objectives. On this point please see *R. (on the application of Bristol City Council) v Bristol Magistrates Court & Somerfield Stores Ltd* (2009) L.L.R. 333 referred to later in this chapter.

Of course, the licensing authority must, where relevant, attach the mandatory conditions (ss.19–21) and avoid the prohibited condition (s.22).

In addition to the requirements of the Act, there are certain principles of condition-making that need to be borne in mind.

8.2   Principles of condition-making

8.2.1   *Conditions must be reasonable*

In *Associated Provincial Picture Houses v Wednesbury Corporation* (1948), in relation to licence conditions, the court indicated in the matter of licence conditions that they should be reasonable, in respect of the use of the licensed premises and in the public interest.

8.2.2   *Any condition must be capable of being directly complied with by the licensee*

For example, a condition requiring a licensee to keep noise to a certain level would be intra vires because the licensee has control over the level at which the music is set.

On the other hand, a condition requiring patrons to leave the area quietly would be ultra vires because the licensee has no direct control over patrons' behaviour once they leave his premises. However, if patrons did cause a nuisance then it would be lawful to refuse a licence, or to restrict hours to prevent such a nuisance.

In *Lidster v Owen* (1983), the Court of Appeal made it clear that, in considering the grant of a licence, the authorities were 'entitled and bound to consider the needs of the neighbourhood'.

In *Clear v Cynon Valley BC* (1994), where it was held that the behaviour and potential disturbance that may be caused by people on their way to premises holding an entertainment licence can be taken into account when setting conditions to be attached to a licence regarding the admission of the public.

Although these judgments were made in respect of previous legislation, the view of the authors is that they are still be valid under the Licensing Act 2003.

Consequently, reasonable conditions designed to prevent disturbance to residents are perfectly acceptable, providing they are within the licensee's power. For example, a condition could be attached to premises requiring door staff to ask patrons to leave quietly while they are still on the premises.

8.2.3 Conditions cannot be used to achieve an ulterior motive outside the purpose of the enabling legislation

See *Pyx Granite Company Ltd v Minister of Housing and Local Government* (1958). Consequently, a condition requiring a premises licence to have valid planning permission would be ultra vires because planning is not one of the purposes of the Licensing Act 2003.

8.2.4 A licence condition cannot override primary legislation

For example, a condition censoring the content of a play, except on safety grounds, would be unlawful because of the provisions of s.22.

8.2.5 Conditions and the operating Schedule

In *R. (on the application of Bristol City Council) v Bristol Magistrates Court & Somerfield Stores Ltd* (2009) L.L.R. 333. The court held

(1) No statutory provision in the 2003 Act incorporates the Operating Schedule into the premises licence. The prescribed application form does not require an application to be granted in accordance with the operating schedule. Nor does s.18(2) of the 2003 Act require the schedule to be incorporated in the licence.

(2) Section 18 gives the licensing authority power to impose conditions consistent with the schedule. It does not impose a duty to impose conditions that reproduce the effect of the operating schedule.

(3) It is a criminal offence to fail to comply with whatever the operating schedule contains only if, and to the extent that, what is in the schedule is included in the premises licence ultimately granted by way of conditions. It is the premises licence and any condition which the licensing authority may impose on a premises licence rather than the operating schedule itself which is required to be sufficiently certain to be enforceable.

(4) It is desirable that an operating schedule should describe any steps proposed as clearly as possible so that the authority considering the application are clear as to what it may involve and whether any other steps are required to promote the licensing objectives. If the steps are proposed in a language that is general or opaque the authority may impose a condition describing more specifically and concretely what is proposed if that is necessary to promote

the licensing objectives. Such a condition would be consistent with the operating schedule—it would just be more specific

(5) Apart from the Mandatory Conditions there is no obligation on the Licensing Authority to impose conditions

(6) There is no duty to impose conditions to ensure the operator complies with the objectives if other legislation will ensure compliance.

8.2.6 *Conditions should be clear and understandable*

In *R. v Hammersmith and Fulham LBC Ex p. Earls Court Ltd* (1993), the court took the view that any condition 'the meaning of which is so obscure that it necessitates the issue of a construction summons is unreasonable in a *Wednesbury*sense'.

However, **over-generalised conditions** should be avoided. In *Westminster City Council v Blenheim Leisure (No.2)* (1999), the High Court held that the term "good order" was not sufficiently clear. In this case, the court held that the European Convention on Human Rights requires all matters which could lead to a criminal offence being committed to be spelt out clearly.

In *R. (on the application of Westminster Council) v Westminster Metropolitan Stipendiary Magistrates & Merran* (2008) 74 L.L.R. the High Court refused to set aside a District Judge's decision on the basis the conditions as drafted by the District Judge were unenforceable. The High Court agreed the conditions could not be enforced in the way they were drafted but refused to interfere with the Judge's decision that the conditions were sufficient to ensure the Licensing Objectives were complied with so remitted the case to the Judge with suggestions as to how the conditions could be worded.

The decision in *R. (on the application of In The Pink) v Leeds Magistrates Court* (2010) L.L.R. 140 concerned an argument regarding what the Magistrates order meant. While the judicial review was pending the Clerk to the Magistrates wrote a letter explaining what the magistrates had intended to do. The High

Court held that it was better that the clerk had remedied the defect and that there was nothing to be gained from rehearing the matter. It is interesting that in this case the Magistrates had imposed a condition regarding the maximum occupancy of the premises. There was no argument about this condition.

A condition that "All noise arising from regulated entertainment at the premises shall be inaudible 1 metre outside any noise sensitive premises" was quashed by the High Court. The Judge held "Without clarity as to the premises or the location intended to be protected by this condition, and without some degree of specificity as to what is meant by inaudibility the condition is in my judgment so vague as to be unenforceable." (*R. (on the application of Developing Retail Ltd) v East Hampshire Magistrates Court* (March 4, 2011).

Chapter 9

Appeals

9.1 Appeal to the Magistrates Court

The 2003 Act provides for various rights of appeal to the Magistrates Court. An appeal can be lodged against a decision to refuse an application for a licence/attach conditions to a licence/revoke a licence or attach conditions to it following a review. The parties who can appeal are the applicant who is refused a licence or has conditions attached to an authorisation and any party who made a representation and is not satisfied by the authorities decision e.g. because a licence was granted and the party considered it should not be granted or the authority should have attached various condition to the authorisation and did not do so.

There is also the right of appeal against the decision of a licensing authority to issue a Counter Notice to a Temporary Event Notice (see Ch.5 at p.64). It should be noted that if the police or environmental health authority object to a Late Temporary Event Notice the event cannot go ahead and there is no right of appeal.

On hearing an appeal the Magistrates can:

(a) dismiss the appeal;
(b) substitute for the decision appealed against any other decision which could have been made by the licensing authority;
(c) remit the case to the licensing authority to dispose of in accordance with the direction of the court.

The Magistrates may also make such order as to costs as they think fit.

The licensing authority is always a respondent to an appeal. Where the applicant is appealing against a decision no other party is a respondent to an appeal and it is up to the authority to decide whether or not to call anyone who made a representation as a witness. This point was considered in *R (on the application of Chief Constable of Nottinghamshire) v Nottingham Magistrates Court & Tesco Stores Ltd* (2010) L.L.R. 112. The police had made representations to an application by Tesco's asking for conditions to be attached to a premises licence. The licensing authority granted the licence but attached the conditions requested by the police. Tescos appealed against the conditions. The police applied to the magistrates to be made a respondent to the appeal. The District Judge refused the application holding that under Sch.5 there was no power to make the police a respondent. The High Court upheld the District Judge's decision on this point. However, Lord Justice Moses went on to say that the Magistrates did have a power to regulate their own procedure and did have discretion to allow a party who was not a respondent to make representations to the court. However, the magistrate should determine how best he could do this and achieve a fair result. The magistrate had to bear in mind the different considerations in relation to interested parties and responsible authorities. He had to bear in mind that there was a need to protect the applicant from the undue burden of duplication or arguments. This seems to make it clear that if the District Judge had exercised his discretion to hear the police it would have been done separately from the main appeal hearing.

When a party who made a representation appeals against a decision of the licensing authority the applicant and the licensing authority are always respondents.

Any appeal must be commenced within 21 days of notification of the licensing authority's decision. Under similarly worded provisions in s.300(2) of the Public Health Act 1936 the High Court held that there was no power for the magistrates court to extend the 21 day period for appealing (*Stockton-on-Tees Borough Council v Latif* (2009) L.L.R. 374).

The Court of Appeal considered appeals under the 2003 Act in the case of *R. (on the application of Hope and Glory Public House Ltd) v City of Magistrates Court* (2011) L.L.R. 105. The court confirmed that appeals are a rehearing, new evidence can be introduced and the court must pay regard to the decision of the licensing committee. In connection with this last point the court confirmed the decisions in *Stepney BC v Joffe* (1949) 1 K.B. 599 and *Sagnata Investments Ltd v Norwich Corporation* (1971) 2 Q.B. 614. Toulson J. said "An appeal is a rehearing of which the affected parties are entitled to call evidence and the court must make its decision on the full material before it. The issue is what the proper approach to the original decision, and in particular, the reasons given for it. How much weight the appellate court has to give to the decision of the licensing authority depends upon a variety of factors, the nature of the issue, the nature and quality of the reasons given by the licensing authority and the nature and quality of the evidence on the appeal."

As mentioned above the Magistrates have the power to make an order for costs. However, this power has to be used carefully. The leading case of *City of Bradford Council v Booth* (2001) L.L.R. 151 held

"Where a complainant has successfully challenged before justices an administrative decision made by a police or regulatory authority acting honesty, reasonably, properly and on grounds that reasonably appeared sound, in the exercise of its public duty, the court should consider, in addition to any other relevant fact or circumstances, both

(i) The financial prejudice to the particular complainant if an order for costs is not made in his favour; and

(ii) The need to encourage public authorities to make and stand by honest, reasonable and apparently sound administrative decisions made in the public interest without fear of exposure to undue financial prejudice if the decision is successfully challenged."

This principles laid down in this case have been confirmed in cases concerning appeals under the 2003 Act—*Tower Hamlets LBC v Ashburn Estates t/a The Troxy* (2012) L.L.R. 400; *R. (on the application of Newham LBC) v Stratford Magistrates' Court* [2012] All E.R. (D) 184 and *Saron & Dodds* (2012) L.L.R. 486. In the latter decision the High Court stressed the importance of the Magistrates making a clear decision based on evidence on the issue of whether or not there would be financial hardship if an order for costs were not made against the authority.

The *Tower Hamlets* case concerned costs being awarded where there was an offer of a compromise made just before the appeal was to be heard. The Judge confirmed the Bradford decision when squashing the Magistrates decision to award costs against the authority. The Judge also made an obiter comment about who should make the decision when an offer is made to reach a compromise to settle an appeal. Foskett J. said "It was a committee of the local authority that took the view it did. While it is not, of course, impossible for arrangements to be made to delegate responsibility for agreeing to a different view on behalf of the committee within the local authority structure, it is possibly necessary for the committee to consider some alternative suggestions put to it rather than some delegated individual to do so. This may be the way democracy works. It is clear that counsel for the licensing authority took instructions each time she was invited to do so but it would be difficult to believe there would be someone at the end of the telephone who would have sufficient authority to agree to something less than that which the committee had decided. Again, the question of the consideration of the wider community interests has to be borne in mind in that context."

Although it is a passing comment it makes it clear that if an appellant, or the authority, puts forwards proposals to settle an appeal the matter should be referred to the members to make the decision whether or not to agree to the terms proposed.

Chapter 10

Offences, Closure Orders and Powers of Entry

10.1 Offences

There are a large number of offences set out in the Act in addition to those offences concerning the keeping of the various licences, the display of licences and the production of them.

It is an offence to carry on or to attempt to carry on a licensable activity other than in accordance with an appropriate licence (that is a premises licence, club premises certificate or a temporary event notice), or to knowingly allow such a licensable activity to be carried on.

This offence covers:

- Entirely unlicensed premises, for example, an unlicensed "rave".
- Premises that are licensed, for example for the sale of alcohol, but not for entertainment such as music or dancing but where such entertainment is provided.
- Any contravention of the conditions which are attached to a licence.

The offence carries a maximum penalty of six months imprisonment or a fine of £20,000, or both.

It is also an offence to expose alcohol for sale by retail where there is no appropriate authorisation for such sale in force (s.137). The effect of this provision is that an offence can be committed in a case where no sale or attempted sale is in fact made.

In addition, it is an offence to keep alcohol on the premises with the intention of selling it where there is no appropriate authorisation in force (s.138).

In respect of any of the above offences, a person has a defence if the act or omission was a mistake, was due to his relying on information given to him, was the fault of another person or was due to some cause beyond his control, and he took all reasonable precautions and exercised all due diligence to avoid committing the offence (s.139).

An example of due diligence might be where the premises licence holder of premises licensed only for the sale of alcohol goes on holiday. He appoints an experienced relief manager to deputise for him and leaves clear written instructions as to how the premises are to be conducted in his absence, but the relief manager ignores the instructions and provides regulated entertainment.

Other offences include:

(a)   allowing disorderly conduct on licensed premises (s.140);
(b)   selling alcohol to a person who is drunk (s.141);
(c)   obtaining alcohol for a person who is drunk (s.142);
(d)   the failure of a person who is drunk or disorderly to leave licensed premises when requested to do so (s.141);
(e)   the keeping of smuggled goods on licensed premises (s.144);
(f)   allowing unaccompanied children to be on certain premises which supply alcohol for consumption on the premises (s.145);
(g)   selling alcohol to children (s.146);
(h)   allowing the sale of alcohol to children (s.147);
(i)   the sale of liqueur confectionery to children under 16 (s.148);
(j)   the purchase of alcohol by or on behalf of children (s.149);
(k)   the consumption of alcohol by children (s.150);
(l)   the delivery of alcohol to children (s.151);
(m) sending a child to obtain alcohol (s.152);

(n) knowingly allowing the sale of alcohol by a person aged under 18 (s.153);

(o) selling alcohol on moving vehicles (s.156);

(p) making a false statement in connection with any application under the legislation (s.158).

10.2 Police powers to close premises

Under Part 8 of the Act, the police have the power to close all premises with a premises licence, or in respect of which a temporary event notice has effect, which are located in a particular geographical area, for a period not exceeding 24 hours. The power is exercisable by a Magistrates' Court on application from a police officer of the rank of superintendent or above. It is exercisable only where the Court thinks such an order is necessary to prevent disorder. It is an offence to keep open premises that are subject to a closure order.

A senior police officer (inspector or above) has the power to close specific premises for up to 24 hours with immediate effect. A closure order may be made upon two grounds; the first is where there is actual or likely disorder to the extent that the closure of the related premises is necessary in the interests of public safety, and the second is where closure is necessary to prevent a public nuisance owing to the noise emanating from the premises.

In deciding whether to make a closure order, the police officer must have regard to the conduct of certain defined individuals at the premises. The purpose of this provision is to allow discretion in cases where, for example, it is clear that those managing the premises are treating the disorder or disturbance with sufficient gravity and are taking steps to reduce it or bring it under control.

A senior police officer can extend, in certain limited circumstances, the period for which a closure order may have effect. Such an extension may be for a further period of 24 hours. More than one extension may be made.

A senior police officer can cancel a closure order at any time before it has been considered by Magistrates' Court. Such a cancellation may be made where the officer does not reasonably believe that closure of the premises is necessary because of disorder, likely disorder or because of noise emanating from the premises. The officer must give notice to the licence holder, designated premises supervisor, premises user or manager of the premises where it is decided to cancel a closure order.

After a closure order comes into force, the responsible senior police officer must apply, as soon as possible, to the Magistrates' Court for consideration of the order and any extension by the Court.

The relevant Magistrates' Court, to whom an application has been made, must as soon as practicable hold a hearing to decide whether to exercise its powers. The court has power to:

(a) revoke the closure order and any extension;
(b) order the premises to remain closed or to be closed until the licensing authority has carried out a review;
(c) order the premises to remain closed or to be closed until such a review has been carried out, subject to exceptions specified by the court;
(d) order the premises to remain closed or to be closed until such a review has been carried out, unless conditions specified by the court are satisfied.

Where a licensing authority has received notice from a Magistrates' Court, in respect of a closure order having effect in relation to premises, it must review any premises licence having effect in respect of those premises.

The licensing authority may take steps to further the licensing objectives, including:

(a) revocation of the licence;
(b) modification of the licence conditions;
(c) the exclusion of certain licensable activities; or
(d) the removal of the designated premises supervisor.

The Act makes provision for premises subject to a closure order to remain closed during an appeal against any licensing authority decision to revoke the premises licence (although the licence would remain in force). A Magistrates' Court may order the re-opening of the premises pending the appeal.

In addition to the closure powers under the Licensing Act, the Anti-Social Behaviour Act 2003 gives the police an additional power to close premises where there is the production or supply of Class A drugs and serious nuisance or disorder.

The same legislation also includes a power for environmental health officers authorised by the Chief Executive of the local authority concerned to close licensed premises where a public nuisance is being caused by noise coming from the premises and closure is necessary to prevent that nuisance.

However, it should be noted that when premises are closed under this legislation, the closure orders will not be considered by the Magistrates' Court, nor will a review of the premises licence automatically follow. Of course, it may be that, where a closure order using these powers has been used, the responsible authorities concerned will apply to the relevant licensing authority for a review of the premises licence.

There is a further closure power. Under the provisions of Criminal Justice and Police Act 2001 premises selling alcohol but which are not licensed for the sale of alcohol or which are not operating in accordance with the terms of the licence may be closed by a magistrates court on the application of a police constable or authorised officer of the licensing authority.

A closure **notice** is served on the premises concerned detailing the alleged unauthorised use. The closure notice can then be removed by the police constable or local authority officer where he is satisfied that the necessary requirements have been put in place or, should the activity continue, between seven days and six months after the service of a closure notice (issued by the police or LA) he can apply for a closure order from the Magistrates in respect of the premises specified in the notice.

This power was originally designed to close completely unlicensed premises but because the wording used in the Licensing Act 2003 refers to unauthorised use it now also covers premises operating in contravention of the conditions of the licence.

Some police officers have in the past been under the impression that service of a closure notice meant the premises had to close immediately. This is not the case. A closure notice is merely a first step in a process which could lead to the Magistrates Court issuing a closure order.

10.3   Rights of entry

If a constable or an authorised person (see p.38 regarding authorisation) has reason to believe that any premises are being, or are about to be, used for a licensable activity, they may enter the premises with a view to seeing whether the activity is being, or is to be, carried on under and in accordance with an authorisation (s.179).

A police constable may enter and search any premises in respect of which he has reason to believe an offence under this Act has been, is being or is about to be committed (s.180).

Sections 179 and 180 provide that reasonable force may be used by a police officer or authorised person, if necessary, in order to exercise the above powers. Section 179 also makes it an offence to obstruct an authorised person in the exercise of these powers and it is a criminal offence under the Police Act 1996 to obstruct a police officer in the execution of his duty.

Chapter 11

Early Morning Restriction Orders and the Late Night Levy

11.1 Early Morning Restriction Orders

The 2011 Act introduced a power to enable licensing authorities to make Early Morning Restriction Orders. If such an order is made it will prohibit the supply of alcohol between the hours of Midnight and 6am or such shorter period between these two times as the authority chooses. An authority can only make the order if it considers making it will promote one or more of the licensing objectives. Initial consideration about whether or not to make an order should be undertaken by the Licensing Committee but the final decision must be made by the full Council. If an order is made it can apply to the whole of the authority's area or part of it.

The procedure for making an order will be:

(1) The committee considers if it has sufficient evidence to demonstrate the order is appropriate for the promotion of the licensing objectives.
(2) If the answer is YES, the committee decides on the area, times and if the order will apply 7 days a week or just certain days.
(3) The basis for the proposed order must be put on the authority's website.
(4) Holders of all licences authorising the supply of alcohol in the area covered by the Early Morning Restriction Order must be directly notified of the proposed order.
(5) The authority must advertise the proposed order in a local newspaper and on the authority's website.

(6) People have 42 days to make representations for or against the order.
(7) Representations must be considered by the authority at a hearing of which "good notice" has been given.
(8) If the authority then decides the making of the order is not appropriate for the promotion of the licensing objectives the procedure can be ended.
(9) If satisfied the order is appropriate for the promotion of the objectives the order is made by the full Council. The Council cannot vary the proposed order.
(10) The licensing committee decides on the start date which must be no later than two months after it is made.
(11) The order must be put on the authority's website together with the justification for making it. All affected premises must also be notified and the authority must put up notices in the affected area.
(12) The Secretary of State and neighbouring authorities should also be informed of the making if the order

11.1.1 Exemptions

The order will not apply to sales of alcohol between midnight on December 31 and 6am on January 1.

There will be no exemptions from Early Morning Restriction Orders. There will, however, be provisions to ensure that the supply of alcohol to residents from minibars and room service in hotels and boarding houses is not subject to the Order. The exemption will not apply to residents who purchase alcohol at a bar within the premises.

11.1.2 Late night levy

Sections 125 to 136 of the 2012 Act enable licensing authorities to introduce a levy paid by the holders of premises licences or club premises certificates which authorise the supply of alcohol during the "late night supply period" i.e. beginning at or after midnight and ending at or before 6am. The funds collected will, subject to deductions for the expenses of introducing, collecting, administering and enforcing the scheme, be payable to the police or used by the authority in accordance with regulations. At least 70 per cent of the net amount raised must be paid to the police. The regulations will allow the remaining money raised to be used for other parts of local government which operate or administer measures to address the effect of alcohol related crime and disorder in the night time economy. This could include Street Wardens and the cost of cleaning the highway and relevant land in the authority's area. Highway means a highway maintainable at public expense. Relevant land is defined as land to which the public and entitled or permitted to have access with or without payment and is open to the air.

There will be a discretion for authorities to allow reductions in certain cases.

Proposed discretionary exemptions are:

(1) Premises with overnight accommodation, provided that the sale of alcohol is subject to a condition that, between midnight and 6a.m. alcohol can only be sold to residents for consumption on the premises. The exemption will not apply to hotels and guest houses that serve alcohol to people who are not staying overnight at the premises. This would effect premises holding e.g. a wedding reception which continued after the start hour for the levy and people attending the function were not staying at the hotel.

(2) Theatres and cinemas provided the sale of alcohol is subject to a condition that, between midnight and 6a.m., such sales can only be made to people holding tickets or people taking part in the production for consumption on the premises (where there is otherwise no access to the general public) or to invited guests to a corporate hire event at the premises

(3) Community Amateur Sports Premises will be included as a discretionary exemption from the levy, provided that such premises have relief from business rates by virtue of

being a CASC as defined in Section 658 of the Corporation Tax Act 2010. Such premises include golf clubs and yacht clubs.

(4) Community premises will be included as a discretionary exemption provided the premises have successfully applied for the removal of of the mandatory Designated Premises Supervisor requirement and demonstrated that they can act responsibly.

(5) Country village pubs can a discretionary exemption from the levy subject to specific definitions. In England, the exemption is applicable to premises which are within designated rural settlements with a population of less than 3000. This is the same definition as appears in the qualification for rural rate relief in Part III of the Local Government Finance Act 1988. A rural settlement is defined by a local authority and guidance can be obtained from the Department of Communities and Local Government. This exemption would apply to the sole pub in a rural settlement. Rural rate relief does not apply in Wales. At the time of publication of this book the Home Office is working with the Welsh Government to explore a suitable discretionary exemption that could apply in Wales.

(6) Business Improvement Districts that operate in the night-time economy, with a satisfactory crime and disorder focus will be included as a discretionary exemption from the levy. Licensing authorities will determine whether BIDs in their area are eligible for an exemption. The Home Office will provide more information on this criteria.

(7) Bingo halls open after Midnight for the sale of alcohol can be included as a discretionary local exemption from the levy.

(8) Small business rate relief—certain types of on-trade premises that receive small business rate relief will be eligible for a discretionary reduction from the levy. This will apply to certain types of premises that are in receipt of small business rate relief and have a rateable value below £12000. More information as to the type of premises that will be eligible for a reduction will be included in guidance.

(9) New Year's Eve will be included as a discretionary exemption from the levy. This will mean that if a licensing authority introduce a late night levy premises with an authorisation that allows them to remain open for the sale of alcohol after Midnight on New Year's Eve, will have to pay the levy, unless they apply to vary their licence so the premises close at or before Midnight.

Casino halls with a membership scheme, premises operating under a club premises certificate and restaurants will not be exempted from the late night levy.

11.1.3 *Reductions*

Licensing authorities will be able to offer a discretionary reduction to premises that Are members of Best Practice Schemes e.g. Best Bar None; Pub Watch, Club Watch or Shop Watch. The scheme will have to meet relevant criteria. The criteria will be assessed using benchmarks which will require the Scheme to demonstrate at least the following:

(i)   A clear rationale as to why the Scheme's objectives and activities will, or are likely to, result in a reduction of alcohol related disorder
(ii) A requirement of active participation in the Scheme by members – guidance will be issued as to what active participation could include
(iii) A mechanism to identify and remove in a timely manner those members who do not participate appropriately

Licensing authorities will be able to offer a maximum 30 per cent discount to best practice schemes that meet the specified benchmarks. However, the discount will not be cumulative i.e. a member of Pub Watch and Best Bar None will only receive a 30 per cent reduction from the levy.

11.1.4   *Procedure for introducing the late night levy*

The introduction of the levy enables an authority to introduce the levy in its area where it will apply indefinitely until a decision is made that the levy will cease to apply. The levy period can be set within Midnight to 6am. Unlike EMROs the levy will apply to all the authority's area. There is no discretion to make the levy just apply to e.g. the centre of a town as is the case with EMROs.

In deciding whether or not to introduce a late night levy the authority MUST consider:

(a)   The costs of policing and other arrangements for the reduction or prevention of crime and disorder in connection with the supply of alcohol between midnight and 6am.
(b)   Having regard to those costs the desirability of raising revenue to be applied in accordance with the legislation (s.125(3) of the 2011 Act).

The licensing authority must:

(1)   Discuss the need for the levy with the police and the police and crime commissioner.
(2)   If the authority decides it will not raise enough from the levy to make it worthwhile the decision can be made it is inappropriate to proceed any further.
(3)   If the authority decides to proceed it engages in an initial scoping to decide the design of the levy and considers what services it may fund with the levy.
(4)   The "levy design" is the authority's choice of the late night supply period, the deductions that apply and the proportion of the revenue (after administrative costs are deducted) which the authority wishes to keep to fun other activities related to addressing the effect of alcohol related crime and disorder in the night time economy maximum 30 per cent of the net amount raised.
(5)   The licensing authority make a decision to consult on the design of the levy.

(6)   The licensing authority prepares a consultation document setting out its intention to introduce a levy and its proposed design. The consultation should also consider the services the authority wishes to fund.

(7)   The authority publishes the consultation online, puts the proposal on the authority's website and sends written notification to the relevant policing body, the relevant chief officer of police and all premises licence holders and club premises certificate holders whose authorisations permit the supply of alcohol after midnight on any day

(8)   The notice must set out:
    (i)   the date on which the late night levy is first to apply;
    (ii) the late night supply period;
    (iii) any exemptions;
    (iv) any reductions which will apply;
    (v)   the proportion of the net income the authority will keep.

(9)   The consultation must run for at least 12 weeks.

(10) The authority assesses the responses to the consultation and decides whether or not to proceed with the levy and on its own design.

(11) If it is decided to proceed with the levy the plans are put to the full Council.

(12) The decision to introduce the levy is notified to the Secretary of State and all adjoining local authorities.

(13) The authority notifies all premises with a "relevant late night authorisation" informing them of the start date and giving them a date, not less than two months away, before which minor variation applications can be submitted.

(14) The authority sets the date from which the levy shall begin to apply—this must be three months after the letters are despatched.

(15) The authority publishes on-line an estimate of the costs it will deduct from the levy in the first year.

(16) The levy begins.

11.1.5   *Amount of the levy*

The amount of the levy will depend on the rateable value of the premises. The amount will be is follows:

A   no rateable value to a rateable value of £4300—£299;
B   £4301 to £33000—£768
C   £33001 to £87000—£1259
D   £87001 to £125000—£1365
E   Greater than £125001—£1493

Premises in Bands D and E that are used exclusively or primarily for the supply of alcohol for consumption on the premises will pay £2730 and £4440 per year respectively.

Appendix A

Relevant Offences Under the Licensing Act 2003

1. An offence under this Act.
2. An offence under any of the following enactments:
   (a) Schedule 12 to the London Government Act 1963 (public entertainment licensing);
   (b) the Licensing Act 1964;
   (c) the Private Places of Entertainment (Licensing) Act 1967;
   (d) section 13 of the Theatres Act 1968;
   (e) the Late Night Refreshment Houses Act 1969;
   (f) section 6 of, or Schedule 1 to, the Local Government (Miscellaneous Provisions) Act 1982;
   (g) the Licensing (Occasional Permissions) Act 1983;
   (h) the Cinemas Act 1985;
   (i) the London Local Authorities Act 1990.
3. An offence under the Firearms Act 1968.
4. An offence under Section 1 of the Trade Descriptions Act 1968 (false trade description of goods) in circumstances where the goods in question are or include alcohol.
5. An offence under any of the following provisions of the Theft Act 1968:
   (a) section 1 (theft);
   (b) section 8 (robbery);
   (c) section 9 (burglary);
   (d) section 10 (aggravated burglary);
   (e) section 11 (removal of articles from places open to the public);
   (f) section 12A (aggravated vehicle-taking), in circumstances where subsection (2)(b) of that section applies and the accident caused the death of any person;
   (g) section 13 (abstracting of electricity);
   (h) section 15 (obtaining property by deception);

117

> (i)   section 15A (obtaining a money transfer by deception);
>
> (j)   section 16 (obtaining pecuniary advantage by deception);
>
> (k) section 17 (false accounting);
>
> (l)   section 19 (false statements by company directors, etc.);
>
> (m) section 20 (suppression, etc. of documents);
>
> (n) section 21 (blackmail);
>
> (o) section 22 (handling stolen goods);
>
> (p) section 24A (dishonestly retaining a wrongful credit);
>
> (q) section 25 (going equipped for stealing, etc.).

6.   An offence under section 7(2) of the Gaming Act 1968 (allowing a child to take part in gaming on premises licensed for the sale of alcohol).

7.   An offence under any of the following provisions of the Misuse of Drugs Act 1971):

> (a) section 4(2) (production of a controlled drug);
>
> (b) section 4(3) (supply of a controlled drug);
>
> (c) section 5(3) (possession of a controlled drug with an intent to supply);
>
> (d) section 8 (permitting activities to take place on premises).

8.   An offence under either of the following provisions of the Theft Act 1978:

> (a) section 1 (obtaining services by deception);
>
> (b) section 2 (evasion of liability by deception).

9.   An offence under either of the following provisions of the Customs and Excise Management Act 1979:

> (a) section 170 (disregarding subsection (1)(a) – fraudulent evasion of duty etc.);
>
> (b) section 170B (taking preparatory steps for evasion of duty).

10. An offence under either of the following provisions of the Tobacco Products Duty Act 1979:

> (a) section 8G (possession and sale of unmarked tobacco);
>
> (b) section 8H (use of premises for sale of unmarked tobacco).

11. An offence under the Forgery and Counterfeiting Act 1981 (other than an offence under section 18 or 19 of that Act).

12. An offence under the Firearms (Amendment) Act 1988.
13. An offence under any of the following provisions of the Copyright, Designs and Patents Act 1988:
    (a) section 107(1)(d)(iii) (public exhibition in the course of a business of article infringing copyright);
    (b) section 107(3) (infringement of copyright by public performance of a work)
    (c) section 198(2) (broadcast, etc. of recording of performance made without suffcient consent);
    (d) section 297(1) (fraudulent reception of transmission);
    (e) section 297(A) (supply, etc. of unauthorised decoder).
14. An offence under any of the following provisions of the Road Traffic Act 1988:
    (a) section 3A (causing death by careless driving while under the influence of drink or drugs);
    (b) section 4 (driving, etc. vehicle when under the influence of drink or drugs);
    (c) section 5 (driving, etc. a vehicle with an alcohol concentration above the prescribed limit);
    (d) section 6(6) (failing to co-operate with a preliminary test).
15. An offence under either of the following provisions of the Food Safety Act 1990 in circumstances where the food in question is or includes alcohol—
    (a) section 14 (selling food or drink not of the nature, substance or quality demanded);
    (b) section 15 (falsely describing or presenting food or drink).
16. An offence under section 92(1) or (2) of the Trade Marks Act 1994 (unauthorised use of a trade mark, etc. in relation to goods) in circumstances where the goods in question are or include alcohol.
17. An offence under the Firearms (Amendment) Act 1997.
18. A sexual offence, being an offence—
    (a) listed in Part 2 of Schedule 15 to the Criminal Justice Act 2003, other than an offence mentioned in paragraph 95 (an offence under section 4 of the Sexual Offences Act 1967 – procuring others to commit homosexual activity);

(b)   an offence under Section 8 of the Sexual Offences Act 1956 (intercourse with a defective);

(c)   an offence under section 18 of the Sexual Offences Act 1956 (fraudulent abduction of an heiress).

19.   A violent offence, being any offence which leads, or is intended or likely to lead, to a person's death or to physical injury to a person, including an offence which is required to be charged as arson (whether or not it would otherwise fall within this definition).

20.   An offence under section 3 of the Private Security Industry Act 2001 (engaging in certain activities relating to security without a licence).

21.   An offence under section 46 of the Gambling Act 2005 if the child or young person was invited, caused or permitted to gamble on premises in respect of which a premises licence under this Act had effect.

22.   An offence under the Fraud Act 2006.

22A.   An offence under regulation 6 of the Business Protection from Misleading Marketing Regulations 2008 (offence of misleading advertising) in circumstances where the advertising in question relates to alcohol or goods that contain alcohol

24.   An offence under regulation 8,9,10,11 or 12 of the Consumer Protection from Unfair Trading Regulations 2008 (offences relating to unfair commercial practices) in circumstances where the commercial practice in question is directly connected with the promotion, sale orr supply of alcohol or of a product that includes alcohol.

25.   An offence under section 1 of the Criminal Attempts Act 1981 of attempting to commit an offence that is a relevant offence.

26.   An offence under section 1 of the Criminal Law Act 1997 of conspiracy to commit an offence that is a relevant offence.

27.   The offence at common law of conspiracy to defraud.

Appendix B

Period of Notice for the Various Types of Hearing

Regulation 6 of the Licensing Act 2003 (Hearings) Regulations 2005, SI 2005/44, as amended by the Licensing Act 2003 (Hearings) (Amendment) Regulations 2005, SI 2005/78, requires the following period of notice to be given of a hearing.

In the case of a hearing under:

(a) section 43(3)(a) (cancellation of interim authority notice following police objection); or
(b) section 105(2)(a) (counter notice following objection to a temporary event notice by either the police or environmental health authority),

the licensing authority has to give notice of the hearing no later than two working days before the day, or the first day, on which the hearing is to be held.

In the case of a hearing under:

(a) section 53(A) (summary review of a premises licence) (the timescale for these hearings is set out in s.53(A)(2) of the 2003 Act);
(b) section 167(5)(a) (review of premises licence following closure order);
(c) paragraph 4(3)(a) of Schedule 8 (determination of application for conversion of an existing licence);
(d) paragraph 16(3)(a) of Schedule 8 (determination of application for conversion of existing club certificate); or
(e) paragraph 26(3)(a) of Schedule 8 (determination of application by the holder of a justice's licence for a personal licence),

the licensing authority has to give notice of the hearing no later than five working days before the day, or the first day, on which the hearing is to be held.

In all other cases, the licensing authority has to give notice of the hearing no later than ten working days before the day, or the first day, on which the hearing is to be held.

Appendix C

The period of time within which a hearing must be commenced

Regulation 5 of the Licensing Act 2003 (Hearings) Regulations 2005 as amended by the Licensing Act 2003 (Hearings) (Amendment) Regulations 2005.

Schedule 1

	Column 1	Column 2
	Provision under which hearing is held.	**Period of time within which hearing must be commenced.**
1.	Section 18(3)(a) (determination of application for premises licence).	20 working days beginning with the day after the end of the period during which representations may be made as prescribed under section 17(5)(c).
2.	Section 31(3)(a) (determination of application for a provisional statement).	20 working days beginning with the day after the end of the period during which representations may be made as prescribed under section 17(5)(c) by virtue of section 30.

3.	Section 35(3)(a) (determination of application to vary premises licence).	20 working days beginning with the day after the end of the period during which representations may be made as prescribed under section 17(5)(c) by virtue of section 34(5).
4.	Section 39(3)(a) (determination of application to vary premises licence to specify individual as premises supervisor).	20 working days beginning with the day after the end of the period within which a chief officer of police may give notice under section 37(5).
5.	Section 44(5)(a) (determination of application for transfer of premises licence).	20 working days beginning with the day after the end of the period within which a chief officer of police may give notice under section 42(6).
6.	Section 48(3)(a) (cancellation of interim authority notice following police objection).	5 working days beginning with the day after the end of the period within which a chief officer of police may give notice under section 48(2).

7.	Section 53(A)2 (determination of an Application for a summary review	**(a)** 48 hours from receipt of an application the authority must consider whether or not to take any interim steps **(b)** within 28 days of receipt of the application
8.	Section 52(2) (determination of application for review of premises licence).	20 working days beginning with the day after the end of the period during which representations may be made as prescribed under section 51(3)(c).
9.	Section 72(3)(a) (determination of application for club premises certificate).	20 working days beginning with the day after the end of the period during which representations may be made as prescribed under section 71(6)(c).
10.	Section 85(3) (determination of application to vary club premises certificate).	20 working days beginning with the day after the end of the period during which representations may be made as prescribed under section 71(6)(c) by virtue of section 84(4).
11.	Section 88(2) (determination of application for review of club premises certificate).	20 working days beginning with the day after the end of the period during which representations may be made as prescribed under section 87(3)(c).

12.	Section 105(2)(a) (counter notice following police or environmental health authority objection to temporary event notice).	7 working days beginning with the day after the end of the period within which a chief officer of police may give a notice under section 104(2).
13.	Section 120(7)(a) (determination of application for grant of personal licence).	20 working days beginning with the day after the end of the period within which the chief officer of police may give a notice under section 120(5).
14.	Section 121(6)(a) (determination of application for the renewal of personal licence).	20 working days beginning with the day after the end of the period within which the chief officer of police may give a notice under section 121(3).
15.	Section 124(4)(a) (convictions coming to light after grant or renewal of personal licence).	20 working days beginning with the day after the end of the period within which the chief officer of police may give a notice under section 124(3).

16.	Section 167(5)(a) (review of premises licence following closure order).	10 working days beginning with the day after the day the relevant licensing authority receives the notice given under section 165(4).

Appendix D

The persons to be given notice of a hearing.

Regulation 6 of the Licensing Act 2003 (Hearings) Regulations 2005 as amended by the Licensing Act 2003 (Hearings) (Amendment) Regulations 2005.

	Column 1	Column 2
	Provision under which hearing is held.	**Persons to whom notice of hearing is to be given.**
1.	Section 18(3)(a) (determination of application for premises licence).	**(1)** The person who has made the application under section 17(1); **(2)** persons who have made relevant representations as defined in section 18(6).
2.	Section 31(3)(a) (determination of application for provisional statement).	**(1)** The person who has made the application under section 29(2); **(2)** persons who have made relevant representations as defined in section 31(5).

3.	Section 35(3)(a) (determination of application to vary premises licence).	**(1)** The holder of the premises licence who has made the application under section 34(1); **(2)** persons who have made relevant representations as defined in section 35(5).
4.	Section 39(3)(a) (determination of application to vary premises licence to specify individual as premises supervisor).	**(1)** The holder of the premises licence who has made the application under section 37(1); **(2)** each chief officer of police who has given notice under section 37(5); **(3)** the proposed individual as referred to in section 37(1).
5.	Section 44(5)(a) (determination of application for transfer of premises licence).	**(1)** The person who has made the application under section 42(1); **(2)** each chief officer of police who has given notice under section 42(6); **(3)** the holder of the premises licence in respect of which the application has been made or, if the application is one to which section 43(1) applies, the holder of that licence immediately before the application was made.

6.	Section 48(3)(a) (cancellation of interim authority notice following police objection).	**(1)** The person who has given notice under section 47(2); **(2)** each chief officer of police who has given notice under section 48(2).
7.	Section 52(2) (determination of application for review of premises licence).	**(1)** The holder of the premises licence in respect of which the application has been made; **(2)** persons who have made relevant representations as defined in section 52(7); **(3)** the person who has made the application under section 51(1).
8.	Section 53(A)(2) (determination of a summary review).	**(1)** The holder of the premises licence in respect of which the application has been made. **(2)** The chief officer of police. **(3)** Any other person or responsible authority who has made a representation. **(4)** All other responsible authorities.
9.	Section 72(3)(a) (determination of application for club premises certificate).	**(1)** The club which has made the application under section 71(1); **(2)** persons who have made relevant representations as defined in section 72(7).

10.	Section 85(3)(a) (determination of application to vary club premises certificate).	**(1)** The club which has made the application under section 84(1); **(2)** persons who have made relevant representations as defined in section 85(5).
11.	Section 88(2) (determination of application for review of club premises certificate).	**(1)** The club which holds the club premises certificate in respect of which the application has been made; **(2)** persons who have made relevant representations as defined in section 88(7); **(3)** the person who has made the application under section 87(1).
12.	Section 105(2)(a) (counter notice following police/ environmental health services objection to temporary event notice).	**(1)** The premises user; **(2)** each chief officer of police/environmental health services who has given notice under section 104(2).
13.	Section 120(7)(a) (determination of application for grant of personal licence).	**(1)** The person who has made the application under section 117(1); **(2)** the chief officer of police who has given notice under section 120(5).

14.	Section 121(6)(a) (determination of application for renewal of personal licence).	**(1)** The person who has made the application under section 117(1); **(2)** the chief officer of police who has given notice under section 121(3).
15.	Section 124(4)(a) (convictions coming to light after grant or renewal of personal licence).	**(1)** The holder of the licence in respect of which the notice has been given; **(2)** the chief officer of police who has given notice under section 124(3).
16.	Section 167(5)(a) (review of premises licence following closure order).	**(1)** The holder of the premises licence in respect of which the review has been made; **(2)** persons who have made relevant representations as defined in section 167(9).

Appendix E

The documents that have to accompany a notice of hearing

Regulation 7 of the Licensing Act 2003(Hearings) Regulations 2005 as amended by the Licensing Act 2003 (Hearings) (Amendment) Regulations 2005.

Schedule 3

	Column 1	Column 2	Column 3
	Provision under which hearing is held	Person to whom notice of hearing is given	Documents to accompany notice of hearing
1.	Section 18(3)(a) (determination of application for premises licence).	The person who has made the application under section 17(1).	The relevant representations as defined in section 18(6) which have been made.
2.	Section 31(3)(a) (determination of application for provisional statement).	The person who has made the application under section 29(2).	The relevant representations as defined in section 31(5) which have been made.

3.	Section 35(3)(a) (determination of application to vary premises licence).	The holder of the premises licence who has made the application under section 34(1).	The relevant representations as defined in section 35(5) which have been made.
4.	Section 39(3)(a) (determination of application to vary premises licence to specify individual as premises supervisor).	**(1)** The holder of the premises licence who has made the application under section 37(1); **(2)** the proposed individual as referred to in section 37(1).	The notices which have been given under section 37(6).

5.	Section 44(5)(a) (determination of application for transfer of premises licence).	**(1)** The person who has made the application under section 42(1); **(2)** the holder of the premises licence in respect of which the application has been made or, if the application is one to which section 43(1) applies, the holder of that licence immediately before the application was made.	The notices which have been given under section 42(6).
6.	Section 48(3)(a) (cancellation of interim authority notice following police objection).	The person who has given notice under section 47(2).	The notices which have been given under section 48(2).

7.	Section 52(2) (determination of application for review of premises licence).	The holder of the premises licence in respect of which the application has been made.	The relevant representations as defined in section 52(7) which have been made.
8.	Section 53A(2) (determination of an application for a summary review of a premises licence).	Holder of the premises licence the subject of the application. Any other person or responsible authority that has made a representation	The application given under section 53(A)(1). The certificate provided by the Chief Officer of Police. Other relevant representations that have been made.
9.	Section 72(3)(a) (determination of application for club premises certificate).	The club which has made the application under section 71(1).	The relevant representations as defined in section 72(7) which have been made.
10.	Section 85(3)(a) (determination of application to vary club premises certificate).	The club which has made the application under section 84(1).	The relevant representations as defined in section 85(5) which have been made.

11.	Section 88(2) (determination of application for review of club premises certificate).	The club which holds the club premises certificate in respect of which the application has been made.	The relevant representations as defined in section 88(7) which have been made.
12.	Section 120(7)(a) (determination of application for grant of personal licence).	The person who has made the application under section 117(1).	The notice which has been given under section 120(5)
13.	Section 121(6)(a) (determination of application for renewal of personal licence).	The person who has made the application under section 117(1).	The notice which has been given under section 121(3).
14.	Section 124(4)(a) (convictions coming to light after grant or renewal of personal licence).	The holder of the licence in respect of which the notice has been given.	The notice which has been given under section 124(3).

15.	Section 167(5)(a) (review of premises licence following closure order).	The holder of the premises licence in respect of which the review has been made.	The relevant representations as defined in section 167(9) which have been made.

Appendix F

Meaning of "determination"

Regulation 2 of the Licensing Act 2003(Hearings) Regulations 2005 as amended by the Licensing Act 2003 (Hearings) (Amendment) Regulations 2005.

Schedule 4

Meaning of "determination"

The determination of the authority is the outcome of its consideration, as applicable, of—

1. the relevant representations as defined in section 18(6), in accordance with section 18,
2. the relevant representations as defined in section 31(5), in accordance with section 31,
3. the relevant representations as defined in section 35(5), in accordance with section 35,
4. a notice given under section 37(5), in accordance with section 39,
5. a notice given under section 42(6), in accordance with section 44,
6. a notice given under section 48(2), in accordance with section 48,
7. an application made in accordance with section 51 and any relevant representations as defined in section 52(7), in accordance with section 52,
8. an application under section53 and any representations as defined in section 53A(3) in accordance with section 53
9. the relevant representations as defined in section 72(7), in accordance with section 72,
10. the relevant representations as defined in section 85(5), in accordance with section 85,

11. an application made in accordance with section 87 and any relevant representations as defined in section 88(7), in accordance with section 88,
12. a notice given under section 104(2), in accordance with section 105,
13. a notice given under section 120(5), in accordance with section 120,
14. a notice given under section 121(3), in accordance with section 121,
15. a notice given under section 124(3), in accordance with section 124,
16. the matters referred to in section 167(5)(a), in accordance with section 167,
17. the notice given under paragraph 3(2) or (3) of Schedule 8, in accordance with its paragraph 4,
18. the notice given under paragraph 15(2) or (3) of Schedule 8, in accordance with its paragraph 16, or
19. the notice given under paragraph 25(2) of Schedule 8, in accordance with its paragraph 26.

Index

All indexing is to heading number